Nigel

With my best wishes

David.

6th December 2011

JOIN THE NAVY, SEE THE WORLD?

THE LIFE OF A ROYAL NAVAL OFFICER
1949-1977

by

Lt. Cdr. David Allen, RN (rtd.)

Contents

Introduction	Joining The Royal Navy	
Chapter 1	Britannia Royal Naval College, Dartmouth May 1949 to March 1953 Naval Cadet	9
Chapter 2	HMS DEVONSHIRE April to August 1953 Naval Cadet	17
Chapter 3	HMS TRIUMPH September to December 1953 Naval Cadet	21
Chapter 4	HMS CEYLON January to December 1954 Midshipman	25
Chapter 5	HMS BULWARK January to April 1955 Midshipman	53
Chapter 6	HMS VIRAGO May to August 1955 Sub-Lieutenant	59
Chapter 7	Royal Naval College, Greenwich September 1955 to March 1956 Sub-Lieutenant	63
Chapter 8	Sub-Lieutenant's Courses, Portsmouth April 1955 to September 1956	67
Chapter 9	HMS MODESTE January 1957 to December 1958 Sub-Lieutenant/Lieutenant	73
Chapter 10	HMS SURPRISE January 1959 to September 1960 Lieutenant	109
Chapter 11	HMS ACUTE October 1960 to October 1961 Lieutenant	121

Chapter 12	Interpreter's Course, Paris October 1961 to March 1962 Lieutenant	125
Chapter 13	HMS TIGER April 1962 to April 1963 Lieutenant	127
Chapter 14	HMS MERCURY, East Meon, Hampshire May 1963 to April 1964 Lieutenant	151
Chapter 15	Two-Year Exchange, Australia May 1964 to April 1966 Lieutenant-Commander	153
Chapter 16	Faslane, Scotland April 1966 to June 1968 Lieutenant-Commander	159
Chapter 17	HMS ALBION August 1968 to August 1969 Lieutenant-Commander	167
Chapter 18	HMS ACHILLES September 1969 to March 1971 Lieutenant-Commander	173
Chapter 19	HMS TAMAR, Hong Kong April 1971 to April 1973 Lieutenant-Commander	183
Chapter 20	HMS MERCURY May 1973 to April 1974 Lieutenant-Commander	201
Chapter 21	Kiel, Germany & Karup, Denmark May 1974 to May 1977 Commander	205
Chapter 22	Admiralty Surface Weapons Establishment, Portsmouth, June 1977 to February 1978 Lieutenant-Commander	211
Chapter 23	Career Reflections	215

FastPrint Publishing

www.fast-print.net/bookshop

Join the Navy...
... see the world?

Copyright © Lt. Cdr. David Allen, RN (rtd.) 2011

All rights reserved

No part of this book may be reproduced in any form by photocopying or any electronic or mechanical means, including information storage or retrieval systems, without permission in writing from both the copyright owner and the publisher of the book.

ISBN 978-178035-207-7

First published 2011 by
FASTPRINT PUBLISHING
Peterborough, England.

Acknowledgements

First of all I would like to thank my daughter Catherine who, luckily for me, happens to have her own copywriting and editing business, Canny Communications, in Aberdeen. Her encouragement and effort have played a significant part in enabling this book to reach publication. My eldest son, Brigadier Tim Allen, spent many hours reviewing an early draft and made several valid suggestions for improvement.

Jennifer McAdam (Graphic Designer at the House of Morgan, Aberdeen) used her creative talents to design the front cover and also turned the final draft into the format required by the publishers/printers.

Nelson French provided material about the Spithead Review and the GOTHIC and, as a naval author himself, also much appreciated encouragement.

Last, but certainly not least, I would thank my wife Rosemary for proofing a final draft and not correcting my English as is her wont!

INTRODUCTION

One of my grandchildren, born long after I left the Royal Navy, asked: "What did you do in the Navy, Grandpa?" This gave me the idea that it would be worth recording for the family the type of life a Naval Officer led in the second half of the 20th Century. In my retirement, daughter Catherine and I have spent many hours putting together this little narrative which I hope will be enjoyable and interesting to some, if infuriating to others!

I was born in a rectory in the wilds of Wiltshire where my grandfather was the parson, a lovely country place to spend one's childhood. My father was an Army officer and therefore spent a lot of time away. At the age of seven I was despatched to prep school in Dorset, my mother working in London and my father at the war in North Africa. My grandfather had been round the Horn under sail as a young man but otherwise there was no tradition of the sea in the family.

After the war, my mother re-married and the family moved to Wimborne in Dorset. At the age of 11, my stepfather bought me a half-decked gaff-rigged dinghy, which I kept at the Parkstone Yacht Club on Poole Harbour. The pleasure I gained from this was enormous. I erroneously thought that the Royal Navy would give me plenty of opportunity to pursue my hobby, so, at the age of thirteen, I volunteered. My mother encouraged me; I am sure she was wondering how she was going to pay Sherborne's school fees. Dartmouth's fees, in comparison, were only £20 per term, clearly heavily subsidised.

In 1949 the process for joining the Royal Navy as a cadet had changed little since Nelson's time. The written exam, very similar to the Common Entrance to public schools, whittled the original 1,200 applicants to some 200. The survivors had to report to Queen Anne's Mansions in St James, London for an interview and medical. My mother very thoughtfully arranged for a distant cousin, Engineering Admiral Brian Sebastian, to coach me in interview techniques. The standard questions were known to be: Why you do want to join the Navy? What do you hope to achieve as a naval officer? Have you been aboard a Royal Navy ship?

The Interview Board consisted of a row of uniformed admirals and three civilians of unknown origin, pretty intimidating for a small boy aged thirteen. Sure enough the standard questions were reeled off and I managed to remember the expected responses. This goes to show that, while there may be plenty of "who you know in this world rather than what you know", thorough preparation for an interview pays off.

Many quirky traditions still abounded in the Royal Navy at that time. For example, I first knew I had been accepted when the naval tailors, Messrs Gieves, invited me to go to London for a fitting, a doeskin reefer jacket and greatcoat in particular. This was to be the last officer entry into the Royal Navy at the age of thirteen, so I was also making a little bit of history.

Chapter 1
Britannia Royal Naval College, Dartmouth
May 1949 to March 1953
Naval Cadet

Cadet Allen at Clevedon Lodge, Wimborne, April 1949

In April 1949, I was one of a group of 16 very apprehensive 13-year old boys who arrived at Kingswear station, across the river from Dartmouth. We were met by a Chief Petty Officer who was very quick to put everyone at their ease. We had arrived two days in advance of the main body of cadets, some 600 odd.

For the first year we lived in a house separate from the rest of the College. The House Officer was a distinguished wartime Motor

Torpedo Boat captain, Denis Jermain. Most of us did not realise how this mild-mannered man had caused such havoc to enemy shipping in the Mediterranean and the Channel.

We lived in dormitories which were known as "chestflats". In fact they contained just ancient naval chests and beds. All our clothing had to be laid out for inspection on these chests every evening. One large room was set aside for recreation but there wasn't much time for that.

To describe life at Dartmouth, I can't do better than quote from a near contemporary Admiral Guy Liardet's article in "The Times" (March 2009):

"Admiral Sir Frank Twiss is often credited with the wry jest that life at the Royal Naval College at Dartmouth was excellent preparation for a prisoner-of-war camp. What he actually meant was that the training at Dartmouth, while certainly fairly rugged, "imbued officers with tenacity, esprit de corps and a concern never to let the side down or to do anything that would bring disrepute to the Navy or to your ship"....Up to 1949, entry [to Dartmouth] had been at 13, and was, naturally, formative. Cadets followed a four-year course, principally educational but with a strong practical flavour, its components ranging from diesel engine stripping through small-boat sailing to ballroom dancing.

Cadets lived in an atmosphere of relentless discipline. Summary justice for untidiness, lack of punctuality and other similar offences was administered by cadet captains (prefects). The college was in all respects a warship, HMS Dartmouth, dormitories were "chestflats"; in a later age a shared room was a "cabin", and one "went ashore" to the local pubs (if you were old enough), though having to muster to catch a notional "liberty boat" before being allowed to do so...."

One of the lasting memories of life at Dartmouth was the truly awful food. Rationing was still on and the lady catering manager had the unenviable task of providing 600 cadets with three meals a day in a central dining hall. I don't suppose a parsimonious Admiralty gave her much money for this purpose. To this day there are several dishes I can't face – baked beans and rice pudding for a start. A trip to a local farm for bacon and eggs on a Sunday afternoon was Mecca.

Cadet Allen, playing fields, Dartmouth

On Sundays a formal parade known as Divisions was held. The Captain inspected usually and it was not good to be picked up by him even for a small matter, like a speck of dust. On Saturday nights much time was spent polishing shoes/boots, a practice not restricted to the Army! After Divisions, the entire College (minus Roman Catholics) repaired (naval expression) to the Chapel for a service. The sound of 600 male voices singing "Eternal Father strong to save" is not something that anyone will ever forget.

As far as I can remember we were paid a shilling (12p) a month. This was usually spent on chocolate at the canteen adjacent to the sports fields. Free time away from the college was very limited, so contact with the opposite sex was pretty rare, though girls were 'imported' from Torquay once a fortnight for ballroom dancing lessons. It was inevitable that there was some homosexual activity, but nothing of a serious nature that I was aware of.

Having been "educated" as a Naval Officer, I have never had a piece of paper to show my academic achievements at Dartmouth. This was just before 'O' and 'A' levels were introduced. Instruction was much the same as at a public school, except that we had to assimilate engineering and seamanship as well. For our last year the brighter members were allowed to specialise in either Maths/Science, English/History or French. I chose French which was taught by a Russian count, a truly inspiring teacher. Grammatical errors were punished by a turn of Cossack dancing in front of the class – a skill I no longer have! I really looked forward to every lesson.

I think it is fair to say that I flourished in this naval environment, and became Head of House for my last term. This gave me lots of privileges, my own cabin (room) for example. In my house the three cadet captains (prefects) formed themselves into a dining club, very unofficial as you were beaten for drinking and smoking normally. On one memorable evening we had managed to get some grouse sent down from Yorkshire by rail and acquired some vintage claret from the town to celebrate my birthday. In the middle of this dinner one of the House Officers, a former Equerry to the Queen, doing his evening 'rounds', burst in upon us. We rapidly invited him to join us. Appreciating that this was living in a style to which he could relate we avoided the normal dire consequences.

Towards the end of my time at Dartmouth the sight in my right eye started to deteriorate slightly. The Captain sent for me and explained that I now was no longer eligible for the Executive (Seaman) branch and could chose either to become a supply or an electrical officer, or I could leave

House Cadet Captain David Allen, 1953

the Navy. He suggested that I take some time to think this over but I declined and straight away informed him that I would leave the Service. I wrote to my mother to explain what had happened. She immediately caught a train to London and camped outside the Second Sea Lord's Office to explain to him the "folly of the situation". Twenty-four hours later the Captain at Dartmouth received an instruction that "Cadet Allen was to remain in the Executive Branch and his eyes were not to be tested for ten years." My mother was not a lady to cross and had clearly succeeded in terrorising the Second Sea Lord! I sometimes wonder what I would have done if I had left the Navy, surely something in the open air, farming perhaps?

During the leaves (holidays) from Dartmouth, I was pre-occupied with sailing my own boat, a sixteen foot, half-decked, gaff-rigged dinghy. With a fellow cadet, we had some success in Poole Harbour and thereabouts. We often won the dinghy handicap races because the Race Officers always seemed to handicap us favourably. My greatest success was to win the Public Schools Regatta in X Class boats in 1951 when it was held in Poole Harbour, local knowledge can be very handy. I beat another local sailor (Jeremy Oakley) who, nine years later, won a gold medal in sailing at the 1960 Rome Olympics!

Passing Out Parade taken by Princess Margaret, Dartmouth, March 1953

Princess Margaret with the Captain, March 1953

Our final Passing Out Parade was taken by Princess Margaret. I had one dance with her. I thought the man was supposed to lead, but not with this lady! So, like all good things, one of the highpoints of my naval career came to an end. From being near the top of the pile at Dartmouth, I went to scrubbing decks in the Training Cruiser....but isn't life like that?

I sometimes reflect how the Dartmouth training and discipline process managed to produce a style of Royal Naval Officer that remained largely unchanged from 1890 to, say, 1960. I wonder whether an over-concentration on discipline and tradition did suppress natural initiative, except, perhaps, among the most rebellious. The most intelligent very often did not progress to the higher echelons of the service, a fact best exemplified by the relatively poor performance of senior naval officers in the Ministry of Defence over many years. Just a thought...

The last entry of 13-year olds to Dartmouth, March 1953 (one having already left)
L to R (back): Tom Pearson, Peter Read, Nick Clifton, John Conder, Adrian Phillips, Jeremy McCall, Brian Hortin, (front): John Graham, Tim Hale, Laurie Davies, Colin Traill, David Allen, Simon Fraser, Dennis Davis, Robert Weekes

Chapter 2
HMS DEVONSHIRE
April to August 1953
Naval Cadet

Two three-month spells as a Cadet in training ships were designed to demonstrate what life on the Lower Deck was like, to enable an officer to understand what sort of experiences a sailor had. Having been pretty well 'cock of the roost' at Dartmouth, to live on a messdeck, complete with hammock and sailor's messing (food), was a substantial change of lifestyle. Scrubbing decks and paintwork was a necessary, everyday task, apparently.

HMS DEVONSHIRE

DEVONSHIRE was a three-funnelled County Class Cruiser of considerable age with 8 inch guns. The ship's sides were very high, giving a very splendid rolling motion in a seaway. The masts were metal single poles with yardarms over 100 feet above the steel deck. After an outing up these armed with a bucket and scrubber, I decided that this was not something I enjoyed too much. Fortunately, we had those who really liked this activity, usually Australians, so I avoided volunteering. At this time the Royal Navy was training Cadets of several nations, Australia, Canada, India, Pakistan and Sri Lanka.

As a training ship, except for seamanship and engineering, the DEVONSHIRE's equipment was too outdated to be professionally very useful. However it did have huge areas to be cleaned, very good for training I'm sure. The Captain was a distinguished wartime destroyer captain and kept his labrador on board.

We had a summer cruise to Norway, visiting two of the more spectacular fjords, and Bergen and Kristiansund. At the latter we were invited to a barbecue on the beach to meet the local girls. For shore-going clothes we only had 'dogrobbers' (sports jacket and grey flannels). So off we set armed with towels and bathing costumes. Right at the start the Norwegian girls did what they normally do in the summer, took off all their clothes and charged into the sea! We weren't quite sure what to do but thought we ought to follow suit, which we duly did. You may realise that this is long before the permissive society arrived and so was completely outside our experience. However we coped somehow!

On return from Norway, we spent some time at DEVONSHIRE's home port, Devonport, painting and polishing the ship before sailing for the Queen's Coronation Review at Spithead, off Portsmouth. To be present at the largest assembly of ships – warships, merchant vessels and support vessels – that has taken place, and will probably ever take place, was an extraordinary experience. There were eleven lines of ships at anchor, with the Royal Navy, Royal Australian Navy, Royal Canadian Navy, Royal New Zealand Navy, Indian Navy, Pakistan Navy, Ceylon Navy and 16 other nations present. The USA was represented by the Heavy Cruiser BALTIMORE and the USSR by the Cruiser SVERDLOV. The Royal Navy provided 1 battleship (HMS VANGUARD), 5 Fleet

Carriers, 2 Light Fleet Carriers, 8 Cruisers, 27 Destroyers, 38 Frigates, 28 Submarines and a further 85 other ships, 3 Admiralty Guest Liners, RMV ORCADES – Orient line, RMV PRETORIA CASTLE – Union Castle line, TSS STRATHMORE – P & O line, amongst a large Merchant Navy contingent. The Queen reviewed the fleet from the Despatch Vessel SURPRISE, in which I was to serve later. We gave three cheers as she passed. A very moving moment!

Back alongside at Devonport, there was an outbreak of meningitis on board, and three of our number died. The problem was made worse by the fact that our 'wonderful' medical staff failed to diagnose the disease. My stepfather, a GP, when I told him about the medical staff's inability to diagnose meningitis, wrote to the Admiralty expressing his concerns about their competence. (I learnt later that the officers in question had been retired early). As a result of this, I left an instruction with my mother that in the event of serious illness or injury I was to be moved into private medicine, something I happily never had to invoke.

One of my lasting memories of the DEVONSHIRE was the appalling food, even worse than at Dartmouth. Admittedly rationing was still in force ashore. However we were often so hungry that we used to jump the main course queue and have the pudding first. Then go back and have the main course and a second pudding. Were we meant to understand that sailors always had dreadful food?

To really endear themselves to the next generation of naval officers, their Lordships of the Admiralty decided that the DEVONSHIRE was to be scrapped and that we were to have our second cruise in the light fleet carrier TRIUMPH. What was worse, we the cadets were to transfer all our gear and the training equipment over to the TRIUMPH, and worse still, we were to forfeit a week's leave to do so, with only one week's notice.

One of our number exclaimed: "This is the first time I've missed the opening of the grouse season." Another took even more drastic action and caught a banana boat to the West Indies. On arrival at Trinidad he sent the Captain a telegram:

"Sir, I want to inform you that I am enjoying the sunshine in the Caribbean.

I no longer have the honour to be, Sir,
Your Obedient Servant
Signed...."

From the above you can understand that the DEVONSHIRE didn't leave many happy memories and morale was not great when we joined the TRIUMPH. I questioned in the chapter on the Naval College whether the idea that "I suffered this pain therefore everyone that follows should" was really a very good system for training naval officers of the future. Certainly today's methods are far more cerebral . Of course with Conscription (National Service) still in force, training had to be on an industrial scale.

Chapter 3
HMS TRIUMPH
September to December 1953
Naval Cadet

TRIUMPH was a light fleet carrier, but its aircraft launching and landing facilities had been removed so it was just a big empty ship. With lots of space in the hangars it was very suitable for transporting spares and stores. However, for the time being it was being used for training two terms' worth of cadets, about 200 in all, among their number several Australians, Indians and Pakistanis.

This very large ship, 23,000 tons, was completely unsuitable for training cadets but at least we didn't have to spend pointless hours lashing up hammocks as we had the luxury of bunks to sleep on. The huge area to be kept clean meant that we were required to do just that. Some of us had learnt the tricks of the trade, walking round the ship with a bucket half full of water with a scrubbing brush in it. When stopped and asked what we were doing the reply was: "Going to get clean water". Several of us obtained the key to a small compartment under the flight deck, very handy for skiving (naval parlance) from work.

I do remember an incident during a run ashore in Devonport. My very well-bred compatriot and I decided that it was time to investigate some of the local hostelries. In one pub a local 'lady of the night' when asked by the barman what she wanted to drink replied "a nice port and lemon" at that time considered the tart's drink. My compatriot burst into uncontrollable laughter and we were evicted.

In September 1953 we sailed for a cruise to the Med. After an incredibly rough passage through the Bay of Biscay – the waves actually broke over the flight deck – we arrived at Gibraltar. I remember a rather seedy run ashore to La Linea just across the border in Spain (details too nasty to be recounted here). I put it down to being part of my education! In some respects this was my first 'Jolly Jack' style run ashore.

Our next stop was Majorca, anchoring off Pollensa. I was running one of the boats taking personnel to/from shore but found time to explore the fishing village of Pollensa and its beautiful deserted beach in the September sunshine. This was long before Majorca became a tourist Mecca.

The next port of call was Malta. The cadets were lined up on the flight deck for entry into Grand Harbour and we went alongside at Marsa where the cruise ships go now. The Commander-in-Chief, Mediterranean was none other than Lord Louis Mountbatten, so there was a great deal of pomp and ceremony. However, we lowly cadets were scarcely involved in that. It was my first opportunity to look round this historic and very naval place. More extensive descriptions of Malta follow in Chapter 10. Lord Mountbatten had already had an illustrious career having commanded the South East Asia theatre of operations during World War II and then being the last Governor-General of India.

Virtually the whole Mediterranean fleet sailed to the eastern end of the Med for the fleet regatta at Argostoli Bay in Greece. Every ship from frigate size upwards carried at least one whaler, a 27 foot clinker-built boat, powered either by oars or sail. So for the fleet regatta up to 20 whalers could line up on the starting line. Races were by department, finishing with the officers' race. The Oxford and Cambridge boat race may be a test of endurance but try pulling (rowing) one of these things over a mile. Blisters on hands and bottom were almost inevitable. I can't remember what part I played in this particular regatta.

I do remember going ashore to visit the very basic village of Argostoli with a few other cadets. The only thing of any interest was Ouzo (the Greek pastis), a drink of no great sophistication. We had a few then returned on board. In the middle of the night I awoke with a great thirst, drank some water and was tipsy once more.

After all the traumas before joining TRIUMPH, the three months in her passed without much incident. Just before we got back to Plymouth a notice was put up for us to select where we wished to go for our midshipman's time. Three of us opted for the flagship of the East Indies HMS CEYLON and were granted our first choice. In fact, this was one of the few occasions during my time in the Royal Navy when I was given a choice of appointment.

Chapter 4
HMS CEYLON
January to December 1954
Midshipman

The excitement was intense. After nearly five years' training I was at long last going to join a proper ship. The thrill of all this was magnified by the news that I was to take passage to the East Indies in the troopship Empire Fowey, a former P & O liner, to Colombo in Ceylon (now Sri Lanka). This would be three weeks of some considerable comfort. Being waved off at Southampton by loving parents added to the drama of the occasion. The troopship was full of National Servicemen going to fight the insurgency in Malaya.

The trip out to Colombo provided plenty of interest. There were many firsts for me. We stopped at Port Said at the top of the Suez Canal for a few hours to take on provisions and the Suez Canal pilots. Those master magicians the gully gully men came on board to demonstrate their expertise at sleight of hand, handing you back the watch you didn't know you had lost, producing a baby chicken from your trouser turn-ups and other wizardry.

The passage through the Suez Canal was very special. At that time there were several British army bases alongside the Canal, at Port Tewfiq for example. It was the custom for virtually the whole garrison to turn out and wave a troopship through, accompanied by the usual squaddies' badinage. At times you could see the northbound convoy in the other leg of the Canal. They looked as if they were aground as you could only see their superstructure.

We had a few unaccompanied officers' wives on board but generally speaking the female of the species was a bit scarce. The food was superb compared with rationing in England. P & O ships were largely crewed by Lascar seaman from the Indian sub-continent. The Lascar crew looked after us very well indeed. Our limited duties were usually completed by 10.30am, so it was time for the first gin, lime and soda (gimlet). A certain expertise at bridge acquired at Dartmouth ensured that my bar bill was relatively small, besides gin was only a penny a nip!

We duly arrived at Colombo but only had a day to look round, time to have lunch and a haircut at the Galle Face Hotel, that bastion of colonial life. At this time Ceylon was still a colony and there were a significant number of British living there, mostly tea planters 'up country'.

In the evening we caught the overnight steam train to Trincomalee. If not exactly a comfortable experience, there were only upright seats, it was very exciting. The train was in no hurry and seemed to stop every few minutes or so at a small wayside station. This was my first encounter with the real Orient so there was a lot to take in. The Singhalese girls were very colourfully dressed and the varied smells were something very new. During passages through the thick jungle the sound of elephants trumpeting remains a lasting memory.

HMS CEYLON at Trincomalee

CEYLON was moored at buoys in Trincomalee harbour. On arrival on board we were shown to our quarters. The Midshipmen had a small space traditionally known as the Gunroom for eating and relaxing. There were 20 of us, of whom four were Pakistani. We slept on camp beds in the Midshipmen's chestflat where there were four showers for our use. None of the spaces were air conditioned, so you can imagine the temperature and humidity in a 'tin box' not many miles from the equator!

It had been a tradition for many years that cooks and stewards from Goa served in the East Indian fleet ships. We were very well looked after by our Goanese. On Sundays at sea or at Trincomalee we always had the most superb curry, very hot but a real treat. After lunch a siesta was compulsory!

HMS CEYLON was a Colony Class cruiser with three triple 6-inch gun turrets, two 4-inch mountings and four Bofors. She had originally carried a seaplane behind the bridge superstructure, so had a crane which was very useful on many occasions. The ship had just returned from pounding the Korean hillsides, so in fact the rifling on the 6-inch barrels was worn so smooth that accuracy of fire was very questionable. However it was a beautifully maintained ship, with a teak quarterdeck and Admiral's and Captain's quarters at the stern. The ship was typically commanded by a senior 'four-stripe' captain, doing his last job as a captain or waiting to be promoted rear-admiral.

The chestflat where we slept was infested with cockroaches. One of our number, whose family had a history of alcoholism, awoke everyone one night with a piercing scream. He was looking at an enormous 'cocker' on his chest and thought he had succumbed to Delirium Tremens.

Life on board CEYLON for a midshipman varied between the intensely tedious, socially demanding and occasionally professionally interesting. While at a buoy in Trincomalee harbour, I was responsible along with another midshipman for running the Captain's and officers' fast motor boat (18 knots). It had a twin-screw diesel engine and was a lot of fun to drive. A few of the officers had married quarters on the far side of the harbour, until recently prime Tamil Tiger country, but then very nice places to live on the edge of the jungle.

HMS CEYLON's motor boat

Tropical routine was worked 7a.m. till 1p.m. then lunch and sports, hockey, tennis, football and rugby. Probably illegally, two of us arranged to land on the jungle side of the harbour, with the aim of shooting jungle fowl without much success generally. I know now that these are the birds from which the domesticated chicken evolved.

Perhaps I should explain something about the role of a Midshipman. As an officer under training he was expected to learn as much as possible about the profession of a Naval Officer. We were allowed to have our own bar in the gunroom but alcoholic consumption was strictly monitored. Midshipmen were known as Snotties and the officer in charge of us was therefore known as the Snotties' Nurse.

Midshipmen were supposed to be studying for their examination (Board), though one could hardly say that this was a very demanding task. To aid our studies we were attached to the various departments - Navigation, Communications, Gunnery, Engineering, Electrical and Supply - in rotation. In these departments we were usually given pretty mundane tasks, but at least it was something to occupy spare moments. We also had to keep a Journal to be submitted to the Snotties' Nurse on a weekly basis. This had to contain a page of narrative and a sketch/plan of something relevant. For those with little imagination, poor artistic skills and not great powers of observation this was a horrible chore. Strangely enough I find it quite entertaining to read now. (The map of Trincomalee Harbour (Page 30) from my journal demonstrates these points very adequately).

Trincomalee is one of the largest deep water harbours in the world. In 1954 there were a few naval facilities ashore – sports grounds, a small naval hospital with three real nurses (wow), a NAAFI and canteen, and a jetty big enough to take our resident S-class submarine. The village was a typical mixed race Tamil and Singhalese affair, a few shops, a curry house, a barber, and some ramshackle houses. The tailor made excellent Indian-style shirts, sharkskin dinner jackets, and khaki shorts. The cobbler produced passable suede shoes. The sums charged were pitifully little, but then so was a midshipman's pay, fifteen shillings (75p) a day.

It is obvious from the above that there was very little for the young sailor to do. The tot of rum at 1130 was the highlight of his day. In the evening quite a few returned from ashore legless, or in a very aggressive mood. While Midshipman-of-the-Watch one memorable night, I watched an able seaman returning from shore chasing the 6'3" Officer-of-the-Watch round the quarterdeck. Striking an officer was one of the most serious offences, liable to incur up to 2 years in prison. So we were enjoined to avoid being struck and certainly not retaliate. Hence this rather comic episode. The Master at Arms caught the able seaman and he was confined to cells for the night. Sad to say, many nights the cells were full, usually with the same culprits. So you see binge drinking is not exactly a new phenomenon!

One of the more entertaining features of life in HMS CEYLON was the Somali side party with their jet black skins. They lived in their own mess, so were not seen unless they were scrubbing the ship's side, which they kept in immaculate condition. The Chief Somali was a very rich rogue, all the rest had to pay him a sub to belong to his gang. When visiting other ports, legend had it that the Somalis used to keep bars of gold in their buckets where the customs officers couldn't find them. This was a period when Somaliland was a British protectorate, and thereby enjoying one of its more peaceful moments.

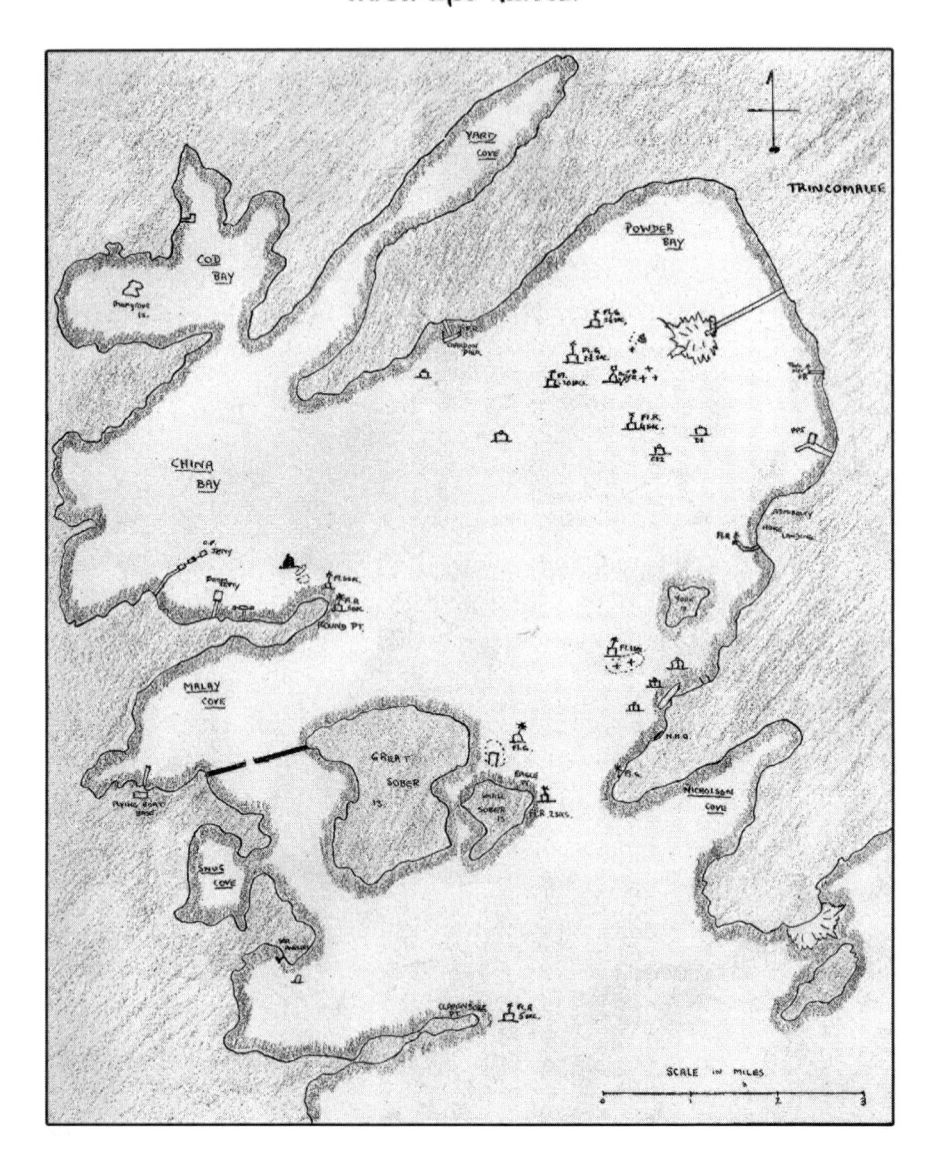

Map of Trincomalee Harbour

CEYLON was not really a very professionally rewarding ship to serve in. In ten months, we had one Fleet exercise lasting four days. My action station was Captain of B turret, the turret just forward of the bridge. The three 6-inch guns were served by a magnificent piece of machinery, the shell hoist, which brought the shells and cartridges up from the magazine four decks below. Fortunately I had a Chief Petty Officer in the turret who knew his drill very well and so my role was really only nominal. We only had one serious shoot but that was very exciting. Firing these enormous shells up to sixteen miles was pretty impressive. While operating off the coast of Korea, CEYLON achieved considerable renown by hitting a North Korean ammunition train providing a night-long fireworks display. That was several months before my arrival on the scene.

So what was CEYLON's reason for being on the East Indies station? Although India had been independent for six years there remained a number of colonies in East Africa, Asia and the dominions of Australia and New Zealand. So the task was to discourage 'adventures' by newly arriving nations which might harm our possessions with independence aspirations beginning to emerge. Showing the flag in far-flung outposts of the Empire was still an important function.

During my ten months in CEYLON, I managed to pay a visit to Madras (Chennai), take part in the Royal Tour of Australia , have some leave up country in Ceylon, enjoy visits to several Indian Ocean ports and take part in an exercise with the Indian and Pakistani navies. Sometimes we embarked the Commander-in-Chief, East Indies, a Vice-Admiral, but most of the time we were left to our own devices as a private ship.

We hadn't been on board long before we set off for Madras on the eastern seaboard of India. We were wondering how India might have changed since independence. The extraordinary thing was that the Indian Civil Service had been so well trained that everything continued much the same as it had in the days of the Raj, at least so I was informed!

On stepping ashore the appalling poverty was quickly apparent and you couldn't fail to notice the smell. There were beggars in the streets. This contrasted with the grandeur of the imperial buildings, such as the domes of the Law Courts. For a first visit to India there were lots of fascinating, but thoroughly uncollectable, items in the shops – brass candlesticks, carpets and so forth. Of course there were several snake charmers playing flutes to their cobras.

From our point of view, the main attraction was a dance laid on by the local Indian army general outside the officers' mess. We were able to disport ourselves in our recently acquired white mess undress – white, 'bumfreezer' jackets, cummerbund and black trousers. The very pretty Anglo-Indian girls thought we were something special, or so it seemed at the time. However opportunities to capitalise on this situation were not available as the last bus back to the ship left at 11pm. Our four Pakistani midshipmen had a problem. The Indians made it very clear that they were not welcome, so they were obliged to remain on board.

While at Madras we heard of the second Comet airliner disaster over the Mediterranean. The Comet was the first jet airliner and was a flagship for Britain. Later metal fatigue was found to be the cause of the crash. From our point of view, we failed to receive our weekly air mail.

On 21st April 1954, we set off for Australia, a ten-day passage across the Indian Ocean to Fremantle. For part of the Royal Tour we were to accompany the SS GOTHIC, a Shaw Saville line cargo passenger boat hired as the Royal Yacht before the BRITANNIA was ready for service. On the way to Fremantle, we carried out our annual full power trial, achieving a speed of 31.4 knots.

In those days Fremantle, the port for Perth, West Australia, was nothing to write home about. It was a lot of warehouses, from where huge quantities of wool and wheat were exported. The town itself was quite small and the shops were very tatty.

Perth already had a population of 220,000, but most of the houses seem to be bungalows with corrugated–iron roofs. There were public parks everywhere with lots of tennis courts. This was of course the heyday of Australian tennis. Australia Day – 55 years to the day as I write – was apparently celebrated with a rowing and sailing regatta, sounds a bit dull by today's standards! I didn't suspect at that time that this was to be the first of many happy visits to Perth, W.A.

The next stop was Norfolk Bay at the southern tip of Tasmania. We spent four days painting the ship from top of mast to waterline. Everyone, including the officers, mucked in from dawn to dusk. At the end, CEYLON looked absolutely magnificent. We were enormously proud to take our very smart ship round the corner to Hobart, the capital of Tasmania.

For the Queen's visit to Hobart, part of the celebrations was to be a rowing regatta at which the New Zealand, Australian and Royal Navy ships would compete against each other in whalers (ship's workboats). So, before breakfast the midshipmen were out practising, resulting in some superb blisters on the hands. Some days later, the standing of the Gunroom was definitely improved when we won the officer's race in front of an enormous crowd.

On 20th February 1954, the Queen and Prince Philip arrived in the GOTHIC.

Boats assembling for Royal Regatta at Hobart

The small port of Hobart provided a very attractive setting with its mainly white houses on the surrounding hillsides. All the naval ships produced street lining parties for the Queen's drive through the town. It felt as if the whole of Tasmania had turned out to welcome the Queen.

HMS CEYLON & HMNZS BLACK PRINCE in Hobart Harbour

I saw quite a lot of Hobart, but from the inside of a motor car. I was 'selected' to drive the Captain's car probably because I was one of the few who had a driving licence (still only just eighteen, I had learnt to drive with my stepfather during leaves from Dartmouth). At that time Hobart was a relatively small town so it was quite difficult to get lost but to understand the Aussie traffic signs was more trying. Anyway it made a nice change from driving motor boats. You might gather that Hobart was a bit of a backwater in 1954. It had the feeling of being a long way from anywhere, which it was. However we thoroughly enjoyed our visit as the people were so friendly.

On 25th February, we entered Sydney Harbour, always a marvellous experience, whether it is for the first time or not. Ahead was the Sydney Harbour bridge, built by British engineering but always known to Australians as "Our Bridge". CEYLON went alongside at Garden Island, Woollomolloo close to the Botanical Gardens and the city centre. So we were really in the middle of the 'action' for a change.

By the time we arrived, the Queen had completed the Sydney part of her tour. That did not detract from the marvellous reception we received

HM the Queen disembarking from the liner GOTHIC in Sydney

from the good people of Sydney. Tennis parties, receptions/cocktail parties, private dinner parties, dances – for a change, the midshipmen had masses of girls ("Sheila's") to choose from. On several occasions the humiliation suffered on the tennis court at the hands of these Aussie lasses was a bit severe, but one of them was the junior champion of New South Wales and went on to win Wimbledon. In pre-permissive society days and at the age of eighteen, I was unprepared for the advances of some of the Australian girls. Somehow I managed to cope!

So what was Sydney like at that time? In 1954 the population was just over a million, i.e. about an eighth of Australia's total population. The shops were pretty ordinary even by UK immediate post-war standards. The city enjoys the most magnificent beaches both to the south of the harbour (Bondi) and to the north (Manley). During our ten-day stay we had plenty of opportunity for barbecues on the beach. Enormous sizzling steaks were quite new for young men brought up on wartime and post-war rationing.

Sydney had a few very special houses – we were invited to several – but a good proportion were red brick bungalows with corrugated iron roofs. Being based in Garden Island dockyard was quite an experience in itself. Merchant ships around us were loading wool and wheat and hundreds of dockies were employed. At 4.30pm the hooter sounded and the dockies converged as one on the pubs just outside the dockyard gate. Why the hurry? The pubs shut at 6pm so, known as "the six o'clock swill", the aim was to down as many glasses of ice-cold beer as possible in the available one and a half hours. As they were turned out of the bars their legs seemed to give way – an interesting spectacle you might say. We regarded that as rather Australian and uncivilised!

The Australian of that time was very proud to be part of the Empire. They were particularly proud of their wartime achievements and quite rightly so. On the other hand they did suffer from an inferiority complex and were not quite sure what Australia's place in the world should be. The thing that struck me most forcibly was the great 'can do' attitude. Also sporting success was very important. I think it would be fair to say that, at that moment, Australia was a cultural desert, with a few cinemas and not much else.

I had a chance to visit a property (farm) a short distance from Sydney. The scale of the place was quite staggering, yet it was pretty small by Australian standards. Life out in the country was pretty basic. The Australian pioneers were very tough folk indeed. After being cooped up on board for many months some of the sailors found the lure of the wide open spaces and the Aussie ladies irresistible - I think we were short of 35 out of 450 when we sailed from Sydney.

So, after a truly memorable visit, we set sail for Melbourne. Although very short of sleep we still had to complete our midshipman's journal. We were just able to get up the river Yarra to berth in the middle of the town. Particularly at that time, the view of Melbourne from seaward was not very striking, the gasometers being the most conspicuous buildings. The Queen left Melbourne to fly to Brisbane more or less as we arrived, so we did not have a chance to see her in Melbourne. I remember seeing pictures of Brisbane in the newspapers. The main street had not yet been tarmaced and there were hitching rails for horses in several places. Rather different from the rows of skyscrapers today.

Melbourne was the city where a large number of migrants settled, especially Italians, Maltese, Greeks and Yugoslavs. So the Englishness of the population was gradually being diluted. The white Australia policy was very much in operation, i.e. only Europeans were allowed in. The policy endeavoured to make the Aborigines conform to the white Australian way of life through schooling, and even forcibly placing Aboriginal children in Australian families. It seems pretty extraordinary and rather bestial to us now.

Wandering around the shops we did not see very much of that. We wondered at the plentiful meat, fruit and veg. Overall Melbourne lacked the excitement of Sydney.

On 18th March 1954, we arrived at Adelaide outer harbour and secured alongside astern of the Orient liner ORONTES. The outer harbour was about 15 miles from Adelaide city centre, about an hour's train ride away. The people of Adelaide had laid on a formidable programme of entertainment for everyone on board including the sailors. Visits to vineyards in the Barossa valley, family homes and for us the Citizen's Ball in the City Hall. My partner for that occasion was a young lady whose family owned one of the best known Australian wineries, she visited us in Salisbury not so long ago.

Myself between two Aussie girls!

After ten days of partying in Adelaide we sailed for Fremantle. We only had one day alongside there because of a polio epidemic. The Queen was not allowed to shake hands which must have been a great relief after the thousands of Australian paws she had already encountered. Fortunately we had already been to Perth, so the disappointment of not having a proper stay was not too great.

The liner GOTHIC alongside at Fremantle

On 1st April we took up station astern of the GOTHIC and set off on the long passage across the Indian Ocean. Trying to keep an exact 2 cables (400 yards) astern of a ship like the GOTHIC, was extremely tedious. It was the midshipman-of-the-watch's task to man the rangefinder and alter CEYLON's engine revolutions "Up 2 turns/Down 2 turns". To do that for four hours required powers of concentration not given to many! A thousand miles to the West of Australia lie the Cocos Islands. The islands were ceded to the Clunies Ross family by Queen Victoria in the late 1800's but by the time of our visit had become an Australian protectorate, with a large airstrip. The Clunies Ross were still very much in charge of activities on the islands.

The GOTHIC launched her two royal barges which promptly broke down. Both the attendant cruisers, CEYLON and NEWFOUNDLAND, officer's boats had been launched for just such a contingency. The NEWFOUNDLAND's boat took the Queen ashore while I followed astern, dressed in No.1W, i.e. up to the neck in full white uniform.

The Queen visiting the Cocos Islands

In May 2008, sitting in a flat in Cannes in the South of France, I was watching a programme about Indian Ocean islands. There was a five second shot of yours truly saluting the Queen as she stepped ashore on the Cocos Islands. An extraordinary co-incidence! So I can add myself to the select few who have visited one of the most remote spots in the world, along with Her Majesty and the Duke of Edinburgh.

Before we parted company with the GOTHIC we had a full ceremonial visit by the Queen to CEYLON. The Ship's company were photographed on the forecastle with Her Majesty and Prince Philip. Then each officer was presented to Her Majesty.

Being presented to HM the Queen

It is interesting to note who was in the royal party accompanying the Queen and Prince Philip:-
Lady Pamela Mountbatten, the Queen's Lady in Waiting
Vice Admiral Abel-Smith, Flag Officer Royal Yachts
Viscount Althorp, the Queen's Equerry (a pupil of my Auntie Gertie, his governess, and to become father of Princess Diana)
Lieutenant-Commander Michael Parker, Prince Philip's Equerry.
(Prince Philip was in the uniform of Admiral of the Fleet).

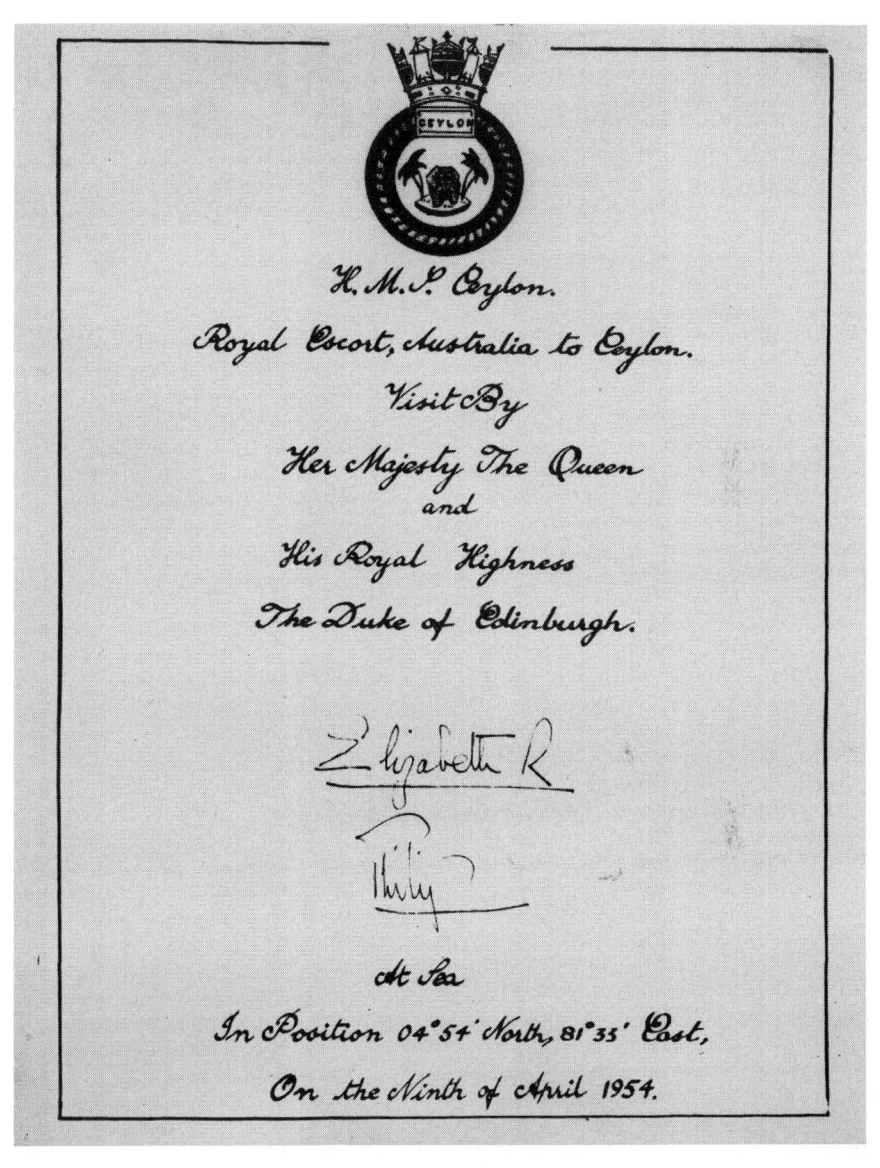

> H.M.S. Ceylon.
> Royal Escort, Australia to Ceylon.
> Visit By
> Her Majesty The Queen
> and
> His Royal Highness
> The Duke of Edinburgh.
>
> *Elizabeth R*
>
> *Philip*
>
> At Sea
> In Position 04° 54' North, 81° 35' East,
> On the Ninth of April 1954.

Certificate affirming the visit of HM the Queen

After the Queen had returned to the GOTHIC we paid farewell to Her Majesty, manning ship and giving three cheers. After leaving we received a signal "splice the mainbrace", a direct command from the Queen. This is the only occasion when officers receive a tot of rum. At the Coronation Review, I was not old enough, so this was my first. Up until 1970 all sailors received a daily 'tot'.

After our Royal Tour 'exertions', we returned to home base Trincomalee. This time we had plenty of opportunity to explore the harbour, sailing trips to outlying beaches and a bit of jungle fowl shooting at the harbour edges.

HMS GOTHIC & HMS CEYLON in the Indian Ocean

Being my usual rebellious self, I asked to have a discussion with the Commander (Executive Officer), a very nice man who went on to become an Admiral and very prominent in naval sailing. I have always needed a project to keep me motivated. I explained that I was bored by the rather pointless existence on board. He was very attentive to my views and persuaded me not to resign. As it turned out I was not alone in my lack of enthusiasm for things naval. More of that later.

My duties consisted of driving the Officer's Motor boat on alternate days according to a strict timetable. When not in use the boat was secured to the ship's boom. To get into/out of the boat one had to walk along the boom about 20 feet above the sea, and then climb up/down the Jacob's ladder. I must have been pretty fit.

One memorable evening my opposite number succeeded in driving the boat onto the only rocks in the harbour at full speed. Somehow or other they got back to the ship and were hoisted out before sinking. Unfortunately it only took the chippies a few days to repair it, so we did not have a very long holiday from boat running.

HMS CEYLON's Gunroom

After a while we were considered due for a week's leave up country in the tea-planting highlands. The rest camp was at an army camp called Diyatalawa near Nureilya. The bus trip up there from Trincomalee, passing through many villages and magnificent scenery, was one of the hairiest I have ever experienced. Overtaking always seemed to occur on blind bends. Do Buddhists seek the hereafter earlier than the rest of us? The rugby team had a couple of outings against the Tea-planters XV. The results proved that they were a deal fitter than we were. No surprise there then!

The tea-planters led a typical ex-patriot life. The Club was the centre of their social life. Most planters were bachelors, but some had found 'housekeepers' from among the Singhalese tea-picking girls.

Some of these lasses were extremely attractive so it was very understandable, particularly as the planters only had six month's leave every three years.

In the middle of May 1954, the Gunroom acquired a new arrival, the Sultan of Zanzibar's grandson. We had had four Pakistanis with us since I joined but this young man was unusual. He was very keen to accord with the sort of discipline we endured and generally was most competent in everything he undertook. His English was excellent.

A Sunderland landing on Trincomalee Harbour

At this time Trincomalee harbour was on the commercial (BOAC) Sunderland seaplane route from London to Singapore. So two or three times a week one of these magnificent machines landed in the harbour, quite a sight. I believe the trip took three days each way, compared with twelve hours today.

On 1st June, CEYLON sailed for a cruise round Indian Ocean islands and East Africa, with more very long sea passages to get there. So this might be a good moment to mention some navigation practices used at that time. This was long before the arrival of the Global Positioning System (GPS) satellites, so celestial navigation was the principal means of determining the ship's position out of sight of land. At dawn, at noon and at dusk the angle of altitude of star or sun or moon was measured by sextant against the horizon at an accurate time. By entering into the astral tables it was possible to produce a position line. So if three or four stars with reasonable arc separation were "shot" within a short interval, a cocked hat or position could be achieved. All this took some time to work out and depended upon a clear horizon. Star sights were one of the more interesting activities for midshipmen; even better if one managed a smaller cocked hat than the navigating officer. I am told that, even with all the electronic aids available today, merchant navy officers are still required to be competent in astral navigation.

The first port of call was Port Louis, Mauritius. As today, this was one of the most exciting places to visit. We had a ship's cocktail party on the first day, lots of very pretty French girls – the French formed eighty per cent of the population then. All my Dartmouth French studies began to pay off and we had lots of tennis and beach parties. The ship's rugby side took on the local French team. The French wiped us off the face of the earth, showing some of the flair their international sides are now famous for. Very humiliating! From a midshipman's point of view this visit was as good as it gets, six days of pure joy. I achieved a long-overdue return visit to Mauritius in 2011.

Next stop was Mtwara, Tanganyika. I have no idea why we spent four days there. All I can remember is that the Royal Marine officer formed a friendship with the local District Officer's wife, the District Officer being away up country! She was on the jetty at Portsmouth a few months later but her husband was not! The best traditions of the Royal Navy continue! One of the midshipmen who came from Kenya left to go on leave at Mtwara. Unfortunately he forgot to return to the ship afterwards. I never discovered what happened to him, as we never saw him again.

Zanzibar is an island Sultanate off the coast of East Africa. It used to be one of the centres of spice trading, and its dhows (lutine rigged sailing boats) are still found all over the Indian Ocean and Persian Gulf. The Sultan was clearly a man of some substance. On his ceremonial visit to the ship he was rowed out in his barge sitting in a seat made entirely of

The Sultan of Zanzibar's barge

silver. His robes were quite spectacular.

We were very keen that the Sultan's grandson should give us a tour of the Sultan's harem. Instead we were taken across the island to one of the Sultan's summer palaces for a swimming and tea party. Zanzibar was firmly controlled by the Sultan in the normal Muslim format, therefore no harem girls, indeed no girls at all, and no beer. However, we were given a reception at the Sultan's palace in the town, a very impressive building.

The Sultan's Palace, Zanzibar

We had time to explore Zanzibar's narrow streets complete with houses with intricate lattice work, some which dated from the thirteenth century. The smell of spices in the market was almost overpowering. (Having visited again in 2011, I am happy to report that it is hardly changed.)

We then moved up the coast to Tanga in Kenya, just a village at that time with a small yacht club for the upcountry expats. We succeeded in losing yet another rugby match, even though by this time we were slightly fitter. By 29th June we had arrived at Dar-es-Salaam, the capital of Tanganyika and residence of the Governor of the Colony. When all this was part of German East Africa they built some impressive buildings. Of course they were "invited" to leave at the end of the First World War. The town was a mixture of ex-patriot buildings and typical African shacks. It was a very prosperous commercial port with many African souvenirs to be had, particularly hand-carved animals.

German Church at Dar-es-Salaam

We played the locals at rugby and lost once more. Then the rugby team hopped on the night train to a place called Morogoro, near Arusha in the Tanganyikan highlands. No sooner off the train than onto the rugby pitch. We won for the only time that I can recollect. The locals, white farmers and game wardens, were delighted to see some fresh faces and the beer flowed freely. Next morning, feeling distinctly frail, we set off on safari. As many modern day safari tours will testify, the country is wonderful. We saw giraffes, many sorts of deer and gazelle, wildebeest, buffalo and herds of zebra. I shot a zebra as the wardens were trying to reduce the number of 'stripey horses'. I think there must have been a shortage of lions; we did not see any. We had a terrific four days at Morogoro, and had no trouble sleeping on the train back to Dar-es-Salaam.

East Africa was not much of a cruise for the sailors. I recorded in my letters home that morale in HMS CEYLON was pretty low, except for the senior ratings who managed to find compatible white mates ashore. By the time we arrived in Mombasa on 7th July it was even difficult to find sailors who wanted to go on yet another beach barbecue. However Mombasa is quite a large port and there was some "talent" for the sailors. The local bar girls are known as "jungle bunnies" and satisfied the requirements of some of the sailors at a price, both financial and medical. The midshipmen had their leave stopped for part of the time at Mombasa. One of our number had advised the Lieutenant-Commander who was in charge of us what he could do with himself. So in the normal naval way collective punishment was imposed!

After Mombasa we sailed for the Indian Ocean isles of the Seychelles, which are very well known nowadays as an upmarket holiday destination. At that time it was a colony virtually unknown to the outside world. I spent most of the three-day visit ferrying people around the islands in my boat. I can still visualise the crystal clear waters, the wonderful fish and the heat. And I hadn't had to pay to be there!

Our young National Service doctor very much took a shine to the Governor's daughter. He was not seen to emerge from his cabin for three weeks after the visit. We were all hugely amused because it seems that he had contracted a sexually transmitted disease very prevalent on the islands! From the Governor's daughter? Who'd have thought!

3rd August saw us back at Trincomalee for a couple of weeks. Most of the Indian and Pakistani navies joined us there prior to a fortnight's exercise. You would not see the Indian and Pakistani navies exercising

Combined fleet of Indian & Pakistani ships in Trincomalee Harbour

together today, but seven years after independence, relations, while not exactly friendly, were not overtly hostile. The exercise itself was designed to practise ship manoeuvring particularly with ships darkened. All the Indian and Pakistani ships were ex RN so were very compatible. The crews had also been trained by the Royal Navy, so signals were well understood. During the two weeks such things as protecting a convoy from submarine attack, defending a force from air attack (the Royal Air Force from Negombo), illuminating ships at night with starshell, were practised. For us midshipmen this was virtually the only naval warfare we experienced in eight months. It must be pointed out that this was real World War II stuff, and bore little relevance to the warfare the Royal Navy was to encounter in the Far East in the years to come.

By the time we sailed for England on 3rd September some members of the ship's company had been on board for 30 months without any home leave. This was completely unacceptable even in those times. The majority slept in hammocks in very confined spaces and the food was uninteresting. I suppose the stoical British wartime spirit continued on. First, we had to sail round the bottom of Ceylon and then west to Aden on the tip of the Arabian peninsula and at the bottom of the Red Sea.

It was essentially a re-fuelling station but was at the time still a piece of the British Empire. From the sailor's point of view it was the cheapest duty free port in the world, so 'rabbits', the naval term for presents, for the homecoming were procured. A real Rolex Oyster was about £20. Anyway all the ship's company had a chance to go ashore and came back laden with goodies.

Then it was up the Red Sea to the Suez Canal. For me that completed transit in both directions. It is always exciting taking a big ship like the CEYLON through. At Port Said at the northern end of the Canal, we had the expected visit from the gully-gully men, the Egyptian conjurors.

Dhows in the Suez Canal

By 20th September we reached Malta. Everyone was keen to make the ship look good on entering Grand Harbour, Valletta under the eyes of the Commander-in-Chief, Mediterranean, Lord Louis Mountbatten. As far as I understood all went well. We only stayed for a couple of days. It was very impressive to see the might of the Mediterranean fleet; there must have been forty or fifty ships and submarines.

CEYLON entering Grand Harbour, Malta

A quick two days at Gibraltar – more shopping – before arriving back at Portsmouth on 1st October. A ship coming home after such a long time away is a very exciting and happy moment. There were several very young children – do not know where they came from! So exciting but also in some ways testing for the families.

The midshipmen were sent on a month's leave. The ground covered in 9 months had been phenomenal. We felt as if we had seen the world, although happily there was plenty more to find. Read on!

Chapter 5
HMS BULWARK
January to April 1955
Midshipman

HMS BULWARK at full power

Although this was only a brief spell of four months there was plenty of incident and interest. We were sent to BULWARK to finish our 16 months as midshipmen and to take the Fleet Board (exam) to enable us to be promoted Acting Sub-Lieutenant, which meant receiving the Queen's commission and the entitlement to carry a sword.

BULWARK was a light fleet aircraft carrier of some 23,000 tons. We went by rail and ferry to join her in Belfast where she was being completed by Messrs Harland and Wolf, very well known nowadays as the builders of the TITANIC. When we joined BULWARK she was doing her sea trials by day and lying alongside by night. One of the sea trials involved winding the speed up to 30 knots under full power, impressive stuff, for a vessel of her size. This was the first time I had served in a new ship.

I well remember the "Mooney's" Bar outside the dockyard gate which had a bar about 30 yards long to accommodate the dockyard workers and their Guinness requirements on their way home. We used to manage about 3 pints, enough to give us some impetus for the following run ashore! The Northern Irish dockers were very amiable drinking companions, no hint of the troubles to come at that stage.

After sea trials the ship sailed down to her home base, Portsmouth. After the commissioning ceremony the ship steamed to Portland for working up and doing acceptance trials for the first naval jet aircraft. When we weren't studying for the Board, viewing these planes landing on and being catapulted off was most exhilarating.

Sea Hawk parked on HMS BULWARK

Sea Venom taxiing on HMS BULWARK

Wyvern being catapulted off HMS BULWARK

However, before BULWARK started these trials, the midshipmen became involved in two unpleasant incidents. The Commander (second-in-command) being a very pukka World War II naval officer, insisted that, whenever flying was not taking place, the ensign staff, a pole of some 20 feet and pretty heavy, was put in place, a pretty tedious procedure. One day the ensign staff disappeared and, because we lived aft in the ship not far from where the ensign staff was situated, the powers-that-be immediately suspected the midshipmen of having disposed of it overboard. We were lined up outside the Captain's cabin and invited to own up. Silence ensued, as this was the first we had heard that the staff was missing. Outside the Captain's cabin I remember saying to the officer in charge of us: "Well, sir, if that is what you think of your midshipmen, perhaps you might consider another ship for us to continue our training". The next thing was that the entire Ship's Company, some 600 personnel, was assembled on the flight deck and addressed by the Gunnery Officer. All leave was to be stopped until the culprits owned up. This statement was greeted by prolonged hissing by much of the Ship's Company, a chilling exercise in man mismanagement. Later that day the four seamen responsible owned up. Needless to say the midshipmen never received an apology.

Until recent times, the Navy has taken a rather dim view of homosexuality. Indeed the most minor offence would become the subject of a court martial, followed by two years in prison and dismissal from the service. This was the norm throughout my naval career. So, imagine our horror when one of our number, an Australian midshipman, was alleged to have been found in a hammock with an able seaman. Apart from the sheer impracticality of this, we didn't believe a word of it as it was so out of keeping for this particular character. However, the witch-hunt continued and the poor lad was shipped back to Australia, where he became a successful chemist on the Sunshine Coast of Queensland. You may be thinking that morale in the good ship BULWARK wasn't that wonderful and you would be right!

After the flight trials the ship paid a visit to Rosyth dockyard. We hoped the navigator had worked out his tide tables correctly, because, even at low tide, there was only a few feet's clearance between the mast and the Forth railway bridge. I was on the ship's bridge as we passed under the bridge, and the calmest person there was the navigating officer. No contact was made, although it looked mighty close.

I had a girlfriend at the time who was doing a domestic science course at one of the 'Colleges for Young Ladies', of which there were many, in Edinburgh. Gathering together a couple of mates we decided that we should pay a visit to ensure that the parents of said young ladies were getting value for their money! So we had a very good party and lock up time (possibly 10pm) came and went. Suddenly 'charge dragon' appeared and we were forced to beat a hasty retreat. By this time we had missed the last train – there was no road bridge then – so we caught a taxi to Queensferry on the south side of the railway bridge. We hitched a lift in the cab of a goods train going across and then jumped off at Inverkeithing as the driver slowed down for us, and walked back to the dockyard at Rosyth.

I didn't take part in the next escapade, but it is so typical of midshipmen's exploits that it ought to be related here. At that time a cabaret artist called Peaches Page used to perform at seaside theatres of which the Empire at Portsmouth was one. Word had got round that she had run screaming from the stage when confronted by a mouse at a showing in the West Country. We noticed that the young lady in question was indeed appearing at the Empire. So a box was hired by a group of 'clergymen' visiting the Portsmouth diocese, a rather unlikely event but the theatre staff didn't seem suspicious. At a suitable moment during Miss Page's performance, a dozen or so white mice descended on parachutes onto the stage. She duly exited stage left, screaming. By the time the theatre staff realised what had happened the 'clergymen' had disappeared.

It wasn't difficult to discover who the culprits were because the escapade occupied the headlines of the Portsmouth Evening News. The Commander-in-Chief, Portsmouth, a gunnery officer with an outstanding war record and a fearsome reputation, summoned the participants to his presence. The assumption was that Easter leave was in jeopardy. The Commander-in-Chief informed them that they had brought disgrace upon the good name of the Royal Navy and that they ought to be ashamed of themselves. Then he said they had brightened up the lives of the people of Portsmouth. At which point the C-in-C's chief steward appeared bearing champagne and glasses!

I am not quite sure how, but I duly passed my midshipman's board, and so became an acting sub-lieutenant.

Chapter 6
HMS VIRAGO
May to August 1955
Sub-Lieutenant

Having passed my midshipman's Board with a second-class pass – not very good – I was appointed to HMS VIRAGO based at Chatham. At that time Chatham was the third naval port after Portsmouth and Plymouth. The object of this brief spell at sea was to enable progress to be made towards obtaining a watch-keeping certificate.

HMS VIRAGO was an anti-submarine frigate, having previously been a wartime destroyer. It had an enclosed bridge and the latest form of submarine detection equipment. So our first task was a NATO exercise in the Iceland-Faeroes gap that lasted two weeks. The wind blew force nine, storm force, virtually the whole time and we had to rig steam pipes on the upper deck to get the ice off the superstructure on a daily basis. World War II was being re-enacted once more! The ship's company were so seasick that the whole submarine detection exercise was pretty pointless. As far as I can remember we didn't make sonar contact with a submarine the entire time, not surprising as the sonar dome would have spent most of its time out of water in the rough sea.

After that fairly harrowing experience, on to nicer things. We were designated as escort for the Royal Yacht BRITANNIA on a state visit to Norway. This was one of the first such visits that the BRITANNIA made. The trip up the Oslofjord in the July sunshine was spectacular. Binoculars were in great demand as the Norwegian ladies were sunning themselves in the "altogether" on the rocks and beaches.

Royal visit to Oslo

British and Norwegian ships at Oslo

On arrival at Oslo I was Officer of the guard for the small RN contingent that King Haakon inspected. I fear my sailors were not at all well drilled compared with the Norwegian navy who had a lot longer to prepare. However all seemed to pass off well, i.e. my captain was pleased!

After this event we went on a short cruise up the Norwegian fjords. A stay at Odda (now regularly visited by cruise ships) was particularly memorable. The scenery – mountains, cliffs and waterfalls – was fantastic. At the inevitable cocktail party I talked to a widowed Norwegian sea captain. He invited me home to supper to meet his very pretty blonde daughter who was a nurse. He clearly was keen that I should get into a relationship with this lass but he poured so much rum down my throat that I nearly needed her professional services rather than romantic ones. I later learnt that our Navigating Officer had not escaped so lightly and ended up marrying a girl from Odda. It is amazing what uses rum can have!

On return from Norway we made a ship's visit to Sunderland. The Mayor and Corporation were invited to the usual reception on board.

HMS VIRAGO under way near Odda

The Mayor, a lady who was as wide as she was tall, charged towards the Wardroom accompanied by the various dignitaries, and promptly occupied all the available seating. The Mayor announced that she was to consume as much as possible as she, a taxpayer, was paying for it. In fact the officers paid for all receptions such as these, and, as it was duty free drink, it didn't cost us much. Her remarks were not well received and I do remember informing the lady, in my usual tactful manner, who actually was paying.

Before returning to Chatham for summer leave, VIRAGO joined the rest of the Home Fleet at Invergordon in the Moray Forth for the Home Fleet Regatta. More torture and blisters in a whaler. We had had no opportunity to train and did not feature in the silverware. My main impression is of the enormity of the Home Fleet as it then was, row upon row of ships from aircraft carriers down to frigates, perhaps forty ships in all.

Invergordon was infamous in the Royal Navy for the mutiny that took place in 1932. The Chancellor of the Exchequer announced in his budget that the pay of the Services was to be reduced by ten per cent. He had forgotten to forewarn the Admiralty so this was the first the Navy had heard of it. The sailors in the whole of the Home Fleet decided to stay below on their messdecks. Eventually their officers talked them out of it, even though they had suffered a similar cut in pay. Could such an event possibly occur again in similarly recessional times?

In those days the pubs in Scotland were only open to 'travellers' on Sundays. So, several of us walked ten miles from Invergordon to Inverness to qualify for a drink. The return trip by bus was much easier. Who would walk ten miles for a drink today?

My four months in VIRAGO was a very happy time. It was a very competent and busy wardroom of nine officers, a charming Captain and at last one had some genuine responsibility.

Chapter 7
Royal Naval College , Greenwich
September 1955 to March 1956
Sub-Lieutenant

In my time, Sub-Lieutenants were sent to Greenwich for two terms to do a course entitled the Junior Officer's War Course, designed to turn these rather crude seafaring folk into human beings. Fat chance! However it was an excellent opportunity to get involved in some of London's social life and the day and night-time pleasures available.

We lived in the magnificent surroundings of the Naval College with its Thames-side position at Greenwich, and famous for its Painted Hall, where we lunched and dined every day. The college is twelve miles from Piccadilly, but public transport consisted then of buses only. Going up to town by car was the obvious choice, parking was pretty easy and there were no breathalysers. A lot of the route to/from Greenwich involved the Old Kent Road, which then had three sets of traffic lights. Coming back at night the challenge was to see if you could make 100 mph down the Old Kent road. Richer Canadian sub-lieutenants had some chance with their Jaguar XK120's. I had a venerable 1936 Riley Tourer which had pre-selector gearing, very good for getting away from the lights quickly but somewhat lacking in top speed. I lent the Riley to a colleague one evening. Returning from an assignation with a girlfriend in Surrey late at night he failed to notice a roundabout. Well, the roundabout was re-configured but the Riley was virtually undamaged.

There were two problems with life at Greenwich. Firstly, we were required to produce a thesis on a selected subject. This involved "work".

I chose antique furniture as my subject for the first term – a good excuse to attend sales at Christie's and Sotheby's, for the entertainment certainly not to buy anything. There was some reading needed, but it was difficult to find the time. Secondly, trying to balance a sub-lieutenant's pay with a playboy's lifestyle was not easy. I remember being sent for by the Commander at the end of one month.

"Allen, do you realise that your pay is less than your Mess bill?"

"Sir, fortunately I have understanding parents and bank manager. I have brought my cheque book." All very embarrassing and showing a slight lack of cash flow control.

A group of us used to 'operate' in London together, going to some debutantes' balls and parties. Some of the girls found much better (and richer) husbands than we would have been, but I like to think we were a bit more amusing with our tales of life at sea. To mention but three of our sometime partners; the top model of the day who married a German steel magnate second time round (Fiona Campbell–Walter), an actress who became a superstar (Susannah Yorke), and a jewellery heiress who became a Duchess (Henrietta Tiarks).

To work off some of the excesses, we had an outstanding rugby team at the College. The fly-half (Mike Pearey) and one wing (Simon Nicholls) appeared for us when they weren't on England duty. The hooker was a Welsh international. How I managed to be selected as prop in this august company, I am not sure. Our opponents were what was then the equivalent of the premier league – Harlequins, Rosslyn Park, Bart's Hospital, London Welsh. We often beat the hospital sides but struggled against the best sides because their forwards were so much bigger and fitter. That winter, during the Army/Navy match at Twickenham, the Navy full-back and Welsh international (Lewis Jones) kicked a penalty from ten yards inside his own half to win the game. I believe that is a record which still stands.

Not much changes over the decades. The pubs we frequented were, typically, the Star in Belgravia (too many guards officers) and the King's Head and Eight Bells near the Embankment at Chelsea (too many merchant bankers). A typical Sunday would consist of downing pints of beer till 3p.m. when the pubs shut. Then off to one of the girl's flats where 'duty' girl had prepared a roast. Not a bad life really.

It is easy to forget that London was subject to the most appalling fog, or smog as it was known, during the winter and spring. The mixture of fog and coal fire fumes was asphyxiating for many with a weak chest. Returning from the West Country one Sunday evening we got as far as Kingston and literally could not see the front of the bonnet. So we pulled the car off the road and left it. We walked perhaps five miles to the nearest tube station. Next evening when the fog had lifted it took us several hours to find the car!

Inter-service rivalry was as active as ever. We mounted an expedition to raid the army at Sandhurst. Security in those days wasn't particularly strong, so in the late night hours of Trafalgar Day we drove in and parked behind the College. We accessed the roof from inside the buildings and exchanged the Union flag for a very large white ensign. We heard later that it was some time before the Union flag was restored; everyone thought the White Ensign was to celebrate some event or other. However the Army retaliated by hoisting an umbrella on top of the Greenwich dome, a feat of considerable mountaineering skill on a roof of doubtful reliability. Cranwell, the RAF College, was too far away to attract our attention, and the 'Crabs' (Navy name for the Air Force) were hardly considered worthy of such an expedition.

One of the highlights of life at the Royal Naval College, Greenwich was Mess Dinner in the Painted Hall, which is one of the most iconic interiors in the country. This wonderful 18th century hall with painted ceilings and walls provided a magnificent setting for dining and balls. The large numbers attending precluded a very refined table but the conversation was always of the highest quality(?!).

Greenwich was an opportunity to savour the delights of London and to develop slightly longer term relationships before we started Sub-Lieutenant's courses based in Portsmouth.

Chapter 8
Sub-Lieutenant's Courses, Portsmouth
April 1955 to September 1956

After a very jolly, largely non-naval time at Greenwich, sub-lieutenants attended a number of professional courses designed to equip them with sufficient specialist knowledge of the many naval subjects in order to be able to carry out any potential appointment at sea. The courses were largely theoretical and involved spending a few weeks at each of the specialist establishments, mostly in the Portsmouth area. At the end of these courses you could volunteer for the Submarine Service or the Fleet Air Arm, if you so wished, or remain in general service, which I chose to do.

Many of the schools were keen to make a good impression on their young charges so that you would want to volunteer for their specialisation, although you didn't have to decide until some years later. Amongst the specialisations were Gunnery, Torpedo and Anti-Submarine, Communications, Navigation, Direction, Fleet Air Arm and Submarines. All of us were Executive Branch (seamen/ship-drivers) first and foremost, so for us these were only sub-specialisations. Engineers, electrical and supply were trained separately.

One's time of promotion to Lieutenant depended to a small degree on the results obtained from these courses, so there was some incentive to do a little work. I really can't remember what level of pass I received at each establishment and in the overall scheme of things only a small proportion of the instruction proved useful in future appointments. These courses were part of the process of moulding one into the naval officer of that era.

The specialist schools were fiercely defensive of their position in the structure of the Navy. However this self-importance did present a number of opportunities for mischievous sub-lieutenants – and there were certainly some of them among my group.

The gunnery course was the most feared of all the courses. It was held mostly at Whale Island, Portsmouth. Apart from the theory involved in making a shell land where it was supposed to, we had long periods on the parade ground, doing rifle and sword drill and practising the art of loading dummy 4-inch and 6-inch shells into the mountings. Some of the more physically inclined enjoyed this course, but I can't say I did. The mindlessness of some of the things we were required to do beggared belief. The climax of the course was an hour-long parade in our best uniforms, swords and medals inspected by the Captain of the gunnery school. Not our group, but a contemporary one, decided that this inquisition was not something to be endured without some form of protest. A few nights before the final parade they had met the managers of the local circus at a pub. They arranged to hire two elephants plus their drivers for the day. Whale Island is joined to the mainland by a single-track causeway. For the passing out parade all traffic across the causeway was halted. So, as the parade was drawing to its end, imagine the scene. Two elephants painted pink for the occasion trundled across the causeway and onto the parade ground. The look of fury on the faces of the senior officers must have been a picture! The perpetrators of the scam suffered a weekend's stoppage of leave, but that seemed a small price to pay for such enjoyment.

For practical firings we spent two weeks at the firing range at Wembury, near Plymouth. Lobbing shells at a target out to sea provided some amusement. In later years when sailing past I always gave that area a wide berth. At Wembury we were accommodated in flimsily-built seaside flats. Scrumpy, Devon rough cider, was available in the local hostelries at 2 pence per pint. Two or three pints produced an incapacity unlike much else. So, after a particularly good evening, we decided to 'invest' in a barrel of the stuff and duly took it back to our abodes. Well, the officer in charge of the barrel failed to ensure that the spigot was properly home. At the conclusion of instruction next day we were met by an extremely irate landlady. The cardboard partitions of her flats had been largely dissolved by escaping cider, something she didn't find terribly amusing, even if we did. So we were moved out into even less inviting accommodation and our leave was stopped until the end of our time there.

The torpedo and anti-submarine course was conducted at HMS VERNON adjacent to the dockyard at Portsmouth. The sonar equipment for detecting submarines was becoming very sophisticated, so we spent a lot of time learning to use various equipment. The same torpedoes which had played such a significant part in winning World War II were in use. They had had only minor improvements made since their introduction many decades previously, and were beautifully engineered pieces of machinery. One of my special memories of VERNON was being woken by WRENs (women sailors) with a cup of tea. Of course we always behaved impeccably!

HMS COLLINGWOOD, the electrical school, was a collection of Nissen huts and tawdry red brick buildings. The electrical branch, 'greenies' as they were known because of the green stripes they wore with the gold at that time, were, I am sorry to say much despised by us seaman officers, a certain sort of naval snobbery you might say. The whole dreary proceedings at COLLINGWOOD clearly needed livening up. At a Mess Dinner as the port was being passed for some reason the lights went out, very embarrassing at the electrical establishment! One of our number had absented himself for long enough to remove a fuse.

HMS MERCURY at Leydene was the home of naval communications, a place I was to get to know well during my Long Course. During the Second World War the Navy set up a chain of radio stations across the world. Before the days of SATCOMS, ship signals were exchanged by high frequency which either hugged the ground/sea or bounced off the ionosphere. To give worldwide coverage, the radio stations were located at all sorts of glamorous places – Mauritius, Singapore, Hong Kong, Australia, New Zealand, Bermuda, Malta and Simonstown (South Africa). It was not lost on me that these were usually commanded by Communications Officers. This seemed to me to be an attractive proposition in the long term, so I took more interest than some of the other courses.

The communications course also involved electronic warfare, the interception of enemy radar and radio signals. The problem was that, so keen was the Navy to keep the enemy (the Soviets) from knowing our intercept capability, the intelligence gleaned was never properly integrated into the warfare process.

The accommodation in many of the establishments was pretty grim. In some classrooms I can remember being so cold that any meaningful instruction could not take place until the coal-burning stove had been going for an hour or so.

One of the better courses we attended was at the Divisional School at the Royal Naval Barracks, Portsmouth. The Navy had always prided itself on man management and probably justifiably so. If you are confined in a ship, often a very small space, with a ship's company of 250 in a Frigate, leadership becomes paramount. The Royal Navy employs a hierarchical system, so that everybody knows where they stand in the order of things and who is their immediate superior. Leadership by example was the key factor, very different from the Army where the soldier has to be taught immediate reaction to orders in the heat of battle. At the Divisional school we were taught the principles and paperwork for managing sailors; these were to stand me in good stead in the Navy and thereafter. Over the years various factors had led to the breakdown of discipline in the Navy. Just to mention one example, during the Royal Tour of South Africa in 1948 the Royal Family were accommodated in the battleship VANGUARD. The whole ship was so focussed on the success of the Royal Visit that the Captain and Officers forgot that 1,500 sailors would also have liked to see something of South Africa, in particular to visit a land where food was plentiful. In short, there was a total lack of consideration for the sailors. In VANGUARD the mutiny took the form of the sailors blockading themselves in the forward mess decks and not coming out until some of their grievances had been addressed. It is worth mentioning that a number of the sailors had been conscripted for 'Hostilities Only' and hadn't been released from the Service three years after the end of the war.

During the Fleet Air Arm course, we had a number of flights from Lee–on–Solent, and were allowed to take the controls some of the time. I remember doing an assisted landing which was quite fun. However, flying did not light my fire!

You will appreciate from some of the previous stories that the social life on Sub's courses wasn't too bad. There were various girlfriends in London who had to be visited over the weekend. Nearly everybody had cars so getting up and down the A3 was not a great problem. The Australians issued a challenge for the fastest time from Hyde Park Corner to the Cosham roundabout, outside Portsmouth, a distance of 67 miles. By the end of the Sub's courses, two Canadians had reduced the time to 55 minutes in a Jaguar XK120.

We had one tragedy. One of our number had an Allard sports car. Returning to base after an evening at a pub he skidded on loose gravel in a country lane and was thrown out of the car and killed instantly. He was a great companion and friend to me, and it took me a long time to come to terms with the loss.

Sporting possibilities were numerous. I played rugby for the United Services Portsmouth Second XV as prop. US Portsmouth provided most of the Navy team. With national servicemen being given preferential appointments the standard was very high and the First XV often beat the best London sides.

At the end of Sub's courses we were all looking forward to going to sea in a proper job. Thoroughly broke after 18 months ashore, we sold our cars and waited for the appointer's letter. I received one to the effect that I had been selected to be an Observer, ie not a Pilot, with the Fleet Air Arm. I replied immediately to say that I had no intention of joining the Fleet Air Arm. Had I wanted to do that I would have joined the Air Force, and they would be receiving my letter of resignation shortly. Twenty-four hours later a phone call informed me I was no longer destined for the Fleet Air Arm but a frigate called MODESTE in the Far East.

Chapter 9
HMS MODESTE
April 1957 to December 1958
Sub-Lieutenant/Lieutenant

Before joining the ship in Singapore, the officers were summoned to the Second Sea Lord's office at the Admiralty. No explanation was given but we were told that we hadn't done anything wrong! On arrival we were told that there had been a mutiny in MODESTE at Aden two months previously. Apparently the First Lieutenant, the second in command in a small ship, had been chased around the upper deck by sailors with meat cleavers. It was explained that our ship's company would be entirely new – not quite true – and that this behaviour was not an inevitable feature of naval life! The ship had been doing nothing very much during the Suez Crisis and the conditions under which 250 sailors lived in non-air conditioned quarters were absolutely appalling, the heat below decks often reaching over 40 degrees.

We flew to Singapore in chartered 4-engine turboprop Britannia aircraft. As Officer-in-Charge of troops, it was my 'duty' to get to know the hostesses over this 3-day flight! The flight was prolonged because the aircraft caught fire over Italy and had to make an emergency landing at Bari. This nearly turned into a "what do you want to do for your last few moments on earth" situation. Finding accommodation overnight for 45 16-year-old boy sailors at Bari proved problematic, but eventually the local brothel proved to have sufficient beds. Some young sailors received an initiation into 'naval life' much earlier than they had expected!

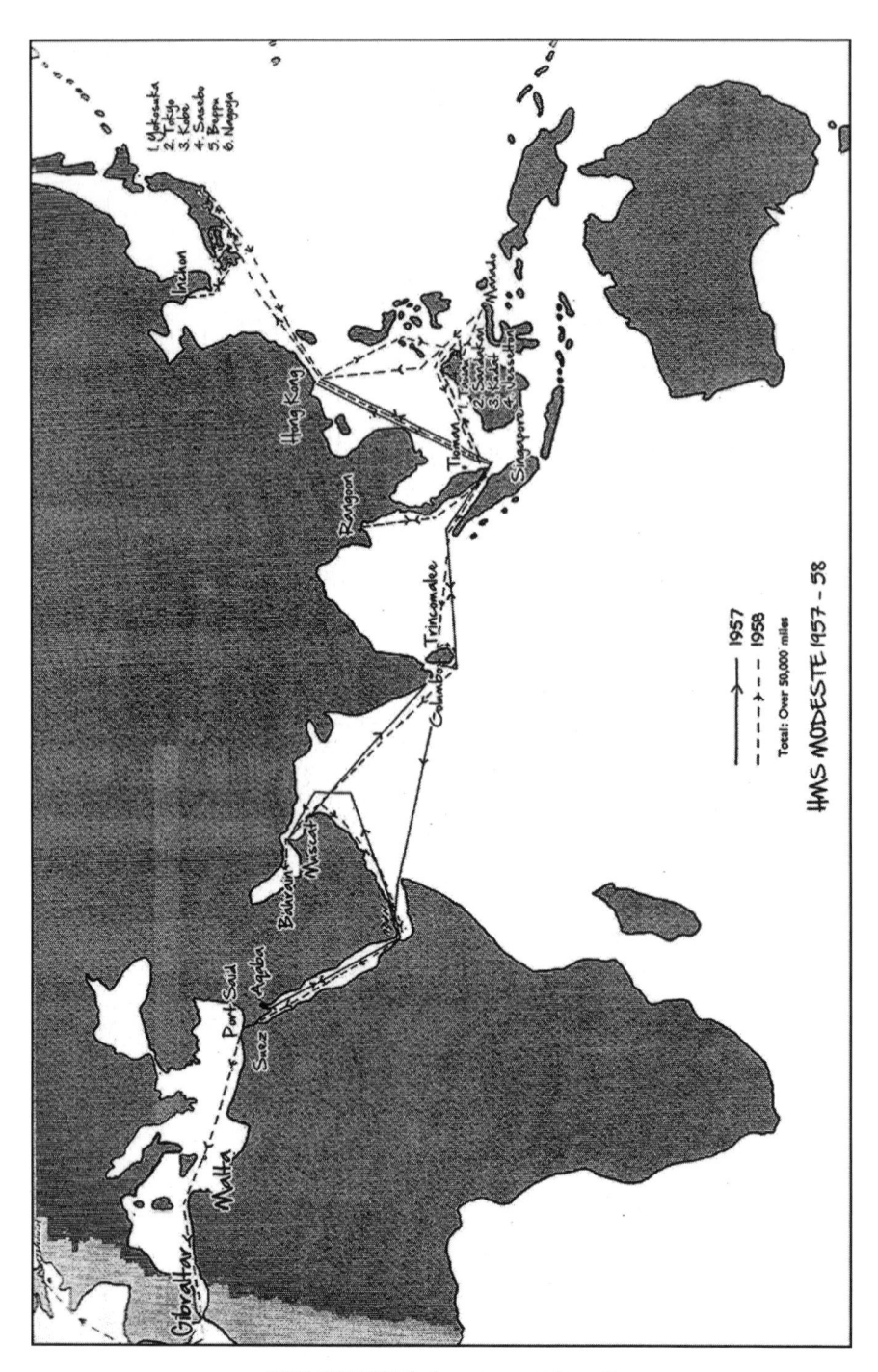

HMS MODESTE's Commission 1957-1958

74 Join the Navy, see the world?

HMS MODESTE at sea off Singapore

MODESTE was a Black Swan-class frigate with three twin 4-inch and six Bofors guns, essentially an anti-aircraft ship, hence the reason for 250 officers and men packed into such a small hull. As a mere Sub-Lieutenant, I was the ship's gunnery officer and correspondence officer, the latter involved looking after the ship's cash.

When we arrived in Singapore to take over the ship we tried to find out why the mutiny had occurred. The ship was laid out with quarters for the ship's ten officers at the rear of the ship taking up a quarter of the hull volume. In the middle quarter, were the engine room and boiler room. The remaining half of the hull was for 240 sailors. In the previous commission the ship's officers had become completely detached from their men who had become out of control, mainly through boredom. The Captain, being of an academic disposition rather than a naval one, barely communicated with his officers. All in all, a real recipe for bad management.

I decided that I would accept nothing on face value when taking over from the previous officers, and asked the base staff ashore to audit everything. By the time these audits were complete the previous commission officers had flown home, which was just as well because the cash account didn't balance due to foreign exchange irregularities. In addition, the Wardroom Mess owed the Royal Hong Yacht Club over £1,000, a great deal of money in those days. The Board of Admiralty invited the previous Captain to settle these debts or be court-martialled. He chose the former!

During the next eighteen months we steamed approximately 45,000 miles and had a most interesting and enjoyable commission. Mostly this could be considered a modern day cruise without the expense!

HMS MODESTE foc's'le

As soon as we had sorted ourselves out on board, we steamed up the South China Sea to Hong Kong for what is known as a 'workup'. This consisted of practising all the weapon systems we possessed. As the Gunnery Officer aged 21, I was responsible for the most heavily armed warship in the Royal Navy (gun per ton). Fortunately the "real"

Gunnery Officer was a most able commissioned Gunner, Peter Hill, who knew what he was doing and was an inspiring leader of men.

Hong Kong skyline 1957

'Junkyard' at Kowloon!

Later on in the commission his expertise enabled us to win the Far East Fleet gunnery competition, beating 39 other ships.

This was my first visit to Hong Kong, a place I was to get to know very well with many visits over the next twenty years or so. In those days it was a relatively undeveloped British colony with an excellent naval dockyard and was incredibly cheap for shopping. Chan Tuck made me two suits, an overcoat, a blazer complete with naval buttons which I still have, and umpteen silk shirts for a sum that even a Sub-Lieutenant could afford, all within a week.

Our stay at Hong Kong was cut short by a few days as MODESTE was despatched to Aqaba, the only port in Jordan, at the top end of the Red Sea. The problem was that there was a crisis in the Lebanon, with all the Arab/Israeli complexities that that entailed. British soldiers were already established ashore in Jordan, but King Hussein needed some protection from seaward. Our task was to provide that and run the port of Aqaba.

When we invited King Hussein on board I volunteered to be Officer of the Guard because I had known the King briefly at prep school.

Self: "Royal Guard ready for your inspection, Your Majesty."

King: "David, I didn't know you were here".

My standing with the ship's company went up enormously, although

King Hussein of Jordan

not perhaps with my Captain, although I had forewarned him.

At Aqaba, for three weeks, two of us did alternate days as Harbourmaster. This entailed making sure that ships coming to collect their phosphate cargo were anchored in a queue according to their arrival time. Yugoslav, Greek, Turkish etc. captains played all manner of tricks to try and get closer to the one and only jetty. The local agent, a rogue if ever there was one, would try and extract "commission" for giving ships a better anchorage. We managed to put a stop to this racket, threatening him with King Hussein if he didn't behave. Mr Mugrabbhi made up for some of his misdemeanours by throwing a Mensaf (Arab feast) on the beach for the ship's company before we left. The Captain had to eat the great delicacy, the goat's eyes! (He didn't know that the Wardroom had engineered this).

Before leaving Aqaba three of us managed to organise a trip to Petra, the "rose red city half as old as time". Carved out of pink rock by the Nabateans, part of the Roman empire, it is one of the most spectacular places on earth. We walked down and came back by horse or donkey, and no charge to visit. Fifty-two years later, there were more like 4,000 visitors and all charged "an arm and a leg".

Temple & prison carved out of the mountain, Petra

Man on camel, Petra

Temple at Petra

The Jordanian Army had a barracks just outside Aqaba. They were still commanded by the infamous Anglo-Arab Glubb Pasha. They took some of us out into the desert which separates Jordan from Iraq to view Bedouin camels and tents. This area known as Wadi Rum was where the film "Lawrence of Arabia" was shot much later.

Bedouin tents and camels

Aqaba 1957

The British Army was being evacuated from Aqaba at the end of our stay with a string of troopships and we provided the escort. The Straits of Tiran at the entrance to the Gulf of Aqaba were extremely narrow and the Egyptians had mounted some guns up above Sharm-el-Sheik. In 1956 we had gone to war with Egypt over the Suez Canal, so as a precaution we went to Action Stations as we passed through. We had live rounds loaded in our 4-inch guns. The Egyptians had manned their batteries but weren't pointing them in our direction. Happily all passed off peacefully.

We steamed back to Aden where we stayed for a few days. It was, as ever, very hot and dry, so we had to make good use of the officers' club beach and refreshments. There was a big drama one day as a shark had got through the shark netting and eaten an RAF child. Well refreshed I am alleged to have said: "better that than a Navy or Army child".

Enough of this lounging around in Aden and off to anti-gun running patrols off Oman. The dhows we searched were capable of 15 knots about the same speed as the MODESTE, so we used to creep up on them in the dark using the radar. And more than 50 years later they are doing much the same - anti-piracy patrols off Somalia!

A not very flattering trial beard

We anchored for a day off Muscat, the capital of the Sultanate of Oman. We inscribed the name of MODESTE on the rocks at the harbour entrance as ships have done for centuries. The Captain called on the Sultan, whom he described as a rather disagreeable old man.

Needless to say we never found a smuggling dhow, although we boarded many. Their crews were delightful, seafaring Arabs. We returned to Hong Kong via Colombo and Singapore for a refit.

To have a three-month period in Hong Kong without interruption was a joy. We moved ashore to HMS TAMAR, the naval base. Meanwhile the Chinese dockies put their all into re-furbishing what was a rather old and well-travelled ship. This was to be the very last refit carried out in Hong Kong Naval Dockyard. The Dockyard was very close to the China Fleet Club where some of the ship's company were accommodated, and to Wanchai with lots of bars and other distractions.

There was a distinct shortage of Western women in Hong Kong at that time. We decided we had to do something to persuade them away from the well-established locals. So we hired a Star Ferry which normally went back and forth between Hong Kong Island and Kowloon on the mainland. We arranged for this ferry to steam around the island from the cocktail hour until the early hours. A band played, fabulous food was provided and we danced the night away. Apparently nobody had thought of doing this before and the evening was deemed a great success. We became well known for this initiative, but I can't say that my social life improved greatly as a result.

I found myself running Navy rugby in the colony. The Army, Police and Hong Kong Club had several regular teams, so the Navy had to select our XV from a rather small catchment area. However, in MODESTE we had a quite passable base for a Navy side with several Navy and US Portsmouth players. There was a small committee who organised the colony's rugby. I can't remember who suggested it but, in October 1957, we held the first Hong Kong Sevens tournament. Teams taking part were: Police, Army A, Army B, Navy, Hong Kong Club A, Hong Kong Club B, and two other privately selected teams. A New Zealand ship, the ROYALIST, was visiting so we managed to put together a fairly formidable Navy Sevens side. We lost narrowly in the final to Hong

Kong Club A, who were mostly Hong Kong and Shanghai Bank and Jardine Mathieson employees. It is strange to think that, from this small beginning, today's international tournament started.

While I was busy enjoying myself I was struck down with amoebic dysentery, a very unpleasant affair indeed. I was shipped off to the naval hospital up the Peak. I am sure the naval nurses were gorgeous but I was in no position to appreciate them. The amoeba are supposed to stay with you forever but I am happy to report I haven't met them since.

What was Hong Kong like in 1957? It was essentially a colony and the Governor decided how it was to be run. Migrants from China escaping from Chairman Mao's purges were pouring in putting a huge strain on the colony's accommodation. The Chinese were very happy to use Hong Kong as the main outlet for trade. Many ex-patriot Brits had an exceptional standard of living as a result. A few Chinese were starting to become exceedingly wealthy, the meld of British rule and Chinese initiative was working very well. Hong Kong was the third busiest port in the world.

Strangely enough the choice for eating out was not that large. One Russian restaurant, one French and any number of Chinese. There was not much culture for eating Chinese, so we often used to eat at the Yacht Club. The food in the Wardroom at TAMAR was of a very high standard provided by our Chinese cooks and stewards. Perhaps we missed an opportunity to eat Chinese food ashore when it would have been very cheap. A propos of nothing at all, the crest of the MODESTE was an upside down rose (see photo of Ship's Company, page 107) which led to much ribaldry at cocktail parties. Obviously a subject that had to wait until the party was well and truly under way !

On 21st January 1957 our long stay at Hong Kong came to an end and we trundled down through the South China Sea to Singapore. Prior to our next visit, which was to Rangoon, as Cash Officer I had to collect a wodge of Burmese currency. The on-board currency was the Singapore dollar so the exchange rate was related to that. My assistant was a national service chartered accountant who later became my best man, Nigel Ayliffe.

Rangoon is situated at the mouth of the Irrawaddy river so navigating amongst the sandbanks was an interesting endeavour. We steamed very slowly using a lead and line over the bows to check the depth as we went. The Burmese are such delightful people, gracious and courteous, that we really enjoyed our time in Rangoon. The enormous golden Schwedagon temple, with the monks in their saffron robes, made the whole scene very colourful. I remember buying large quantities of Burmese cheroots which were very good when fresh. Burma was independent then as the Generals had not yet taken over. I didn't have the impression that the Burmese were any poorer than any other Asians.

Golden Pagoda, Rangoon

Golden Pagoda, Rangoon

At a cocktail party in 2010 a neighbour reminded me that she was in the British Embassy in February 1957 and remembers going on board MODESTE. I regret to say I couldn't remember her.

The officers and ship's company very quickly discovered that by taking Singapore dollars ashore you could get four times as many Burmese Kyats as the "Allen currency exchange" was offering. Fortunately I had recorded how many Kyats each person had exchanged in the first place. So, at the end of the visit I would only exchange back the amount they had exchanged in the first instance. For the surplus Kyats we had a donation box that was used to buy fresh fruit and vegetables. Thanks to this creative accounting the ship's company had enjoyed a 'free' visit! However, on return to Singapore the base staff couldn't understand how I had returned with the same number of Kyats as I started with.

Returning to Singapore for a ship maintenance period I managed to fit in a couple of week's leave. My father, a Lieutenant-Colonel in the British Army, had recently arrived to take command of the Royal Electrical & Mechanical Engineers (REME) workshop. Joined for some of the time by my younger brother, Adrian, who was on his way to emigrating to Australia, we set off for a two-week drive up the East coast of the Malayan peninsula, and back down the West coast. The communist insurgency had more or less ceased, although there were one or two no-go areas.

We stayed at government rest houses and small hotels. A memorable moment was watching giant turtles laying their eggs at night, our visit luckily coinciding with 'turtle-time'. The picturesque Malay houses on stilts and the colourful Malay dress have left a lasting impression. Much remains unaltered today except that now many Malay women wear Moslem veils.

HMS MODESTE's Captain, Cdr. Peter Stuart, myself & brother, Adrian Allen, on Mersing beach, Malaya

Sultan's Palace, Johore

Rubber tapping

Houses at Malacca

Port Malacca 1958

My father was involved in organising Army rugby in Singapore, so an inter-service challenge was an opportunity not to be missed. A New Zealand frigate was visiting so we managed to put together a formidable Navy side, beating the Army comfortably. However, the cricket challenge had the opposite result, so father/son honours ended up even.

HMS MODESTE's rugby team 1958 (I'm front row third from right)

The annual Far East Fleet exercises took place after the maintenance period. The Fleet consisted of three cruisers, five destroyers, four frigates and three submarines. It was not as formidable as it sounds because this was the pre-missile age. All the 'machinery' on display was of World War II vintage.

Guns were very much the prime weaponry. Anti-aircraft fire was tested by firing at a drogue towed by a fairly slow aircraft. One frigate's armament very nearly succeeded in downing the towing aircraft whose pilot was heard to shout over the radio: "I'm towing this f...ing thing not pushing it." MODESTE's Captain lent my father his cabin for these exercises and so young son was able to show off his gunnery prowess.

Life in harbour in Singapore was very pleasant. When not on duty we worked tropical routine. The programme might consist of a swim

HMS NEWCASTLE at speed (note bow wave)

and light lunch at the Officer's club, with copious quantities of Tiger beer, plenty of sport – tennis, golf, hockey, cricket. For the bachelors, there was a small supply of Foreign Office girls, nurses, teachers, senior officers' daughters, but competition for their attention could be quite fierce.

Perhaps this would be a good moment to describe life on board a small ship such as MODESTE. The Wardroom (officers' mess) was quite small with seating for twelve and a bar (open 12 to 2pm, 6pm till whenever) in the corner. We had a Chinese Petty Officer steward, four Chinese stewards and two Chinese cooks. Two officers shared a steward to clean the cabin, do the laundry etc - really a very comfortable existence. The Admiralty allowed us a small sum of money for our food, but that didn't matter in the Far East where everything was so cheap. The cabin in MODESTE was one of the largest I ever had. The Captain lived up forward in a two-room suite (cabin) under the bridge and had his own staff of two. The bridge was open which was lovely in the tropics. 240 sailors shared very cramped accommodation forward. Even the Senior Ratings' messes were very crowded and there was no air conditioning.

This number of sailors was needed to man the magazines, shell hoists, fire control systems and gun mountings.

It was very easy to get into the habit of drinking too much. Before going ashore in the afternoon quite often one had three Horse's Necks (brandy and ginger ale) at three pence each (a beer was sixpence). By playing lots of sport and having plenty of assignations ashore (shopping you understand!), the serial drinking temptations were avoided. The sailors had their rum ration, a neat tot, for the senior ratings – equivalent to two double measures. Junior ratings over 18 had the same tot diluted with two parts water. Junior ratings under 18 received nothing. The ration was doled out at 1130 in the morning and was designed to be consumed with lunch and to keep scurvy at bay. Two cans of beer could be purchased from the NAAFI canteen on board.

While in Singapore I was sent for by the Captain of our Frigate squadron, a distinguished wartime gunnery officer. Because we had performed so well during the recent Fleet exercise he said he would like to recommend me to become a gunnery specialist. I explained that I hadn't yet decided what I wanted to do, but would think about it. I thought that was a tactful way of saying 'no' - though I felt honoured to be so recommended. On 14th March 1958 we sailed from Singapore for Hong Kong. In the Singapore Straits we were diverted to Tawau on the northeast coast of British North Borneo. There had been a coup at the Indonesian town of Manado on the Celebes, Indonesian Islands, and we had to stand by to evacuate 80 British, American and Dutch nationals. So, based in the little port of Tawau we patrolled with police launches at night. Eventually the civilians were repatriated by air.

Tawau became one of the places that I found myself visiting on many occasions. Being situated close to the Indonesian border it was a logging port of some significance, with a District Officer and half a dozen soldiers. They were delighted to have someone new to socialise with.

Eventually we arrived in Hong Kong and joined in an exercise with the Australian carrier MELBOURNE, the New Zealand cruiser ROYALIST and two Australian destroyers. It was quite a change to have Australian aircraft flying around. Our problem was that we had very few communications sets and display systems on board, and certainly no

Copra boat, Tawau, North Borneo

sailors to man them. My memory is that we honestly didn't know what was going on most of the time.

The only air-conditioned space in the MODESTE was the wireless office. One of the wireless operators contracted TB so we had to land him at Hong Kong; sadly he died a week later leaving some nagging doubts about that particular aircon system.

On 8th April we left Hong Kong for a cruise round Japan and Korea. We had been looking forward to this for quite a long time. We were to visit Yokosuka, Tokyo, Kobe, Sasebo, Beppu and Nagoya in Japan, and Inchon and Peng Yong Do in Korea. It reads like a modern day cruise brochure, but we usually stayed for several days at each port and were paid for the pleasure! As a young naval officer who could ask for better! First stop was Yokosuka, south of Tokyo, a colossal American Navy base. The American shopping facilities were superb, so we were able to get all the presents sorted before starting into the serious business of tourism.

On arrival a young American Lieutenant Junior Grade reported on board as the Officer of the Guard. "Gee, folks, is there anything I can do for you?" "Yes. Please arrange to hire a bathhouse for three days for six officers." He looked as if he had been asked to perform mission impossible but returned three hours later with a successful outcome.

So we had a truly memorable three days in the bathhouse – massages, baths, teriyaki, Saki, whisky – provided by the most attentive young ladies. Sleeping on futons was OK provided you had had sufficient Saki. Contrary to popular opinion sexual favours were not on the menu.

At the end of the stay at the bathhouse the following conversation took place:

"Question: Who is going to pay for this lot?"

Very British voice: "Oh, very well then. Pass me my trousers, someone"

Returning on board, I can safely say that I have never seen six more pink and polished officers. All that sunburn scrubbed off!

The Americans looked after us very well, but they lived a very American life on their base and never ventured into the real Japan beyond their gates.

We then moved up the coast to Tokyo, the capital city of Japan.

Street scenes, Tokyo, Japan 1958

Street scenes, Tokyo, Japan 1958

Street scenes, Tokyo, Japan 1958 (note smog mask)

At that time Japan was very far from recovering from the devastation of the war. This was pre-industrial Japan. In fact many of the electrical goods were pretty shoddy. The Japanese Royal Family sat in their palace in splendid isolation and were considered gods. Some of the big department stores – Takashimaya comes to mind – were just getting going. Walking round them was a weird experience because no one spoke English. That didn't matter because most things on sale were so Japanese that one wouldn't want to buy them. The pictures of the street scenes show how little traffic there was, but it didn't stop people complaining about the pollution. The visit to Tokyo taught us how culturally different the Japanese were (are?).

MODESTE's Navigating Officer (Ben Bezance) shopping in Tokyo

Next stop was Kobe which was a great place to visit. The town itself, apart from the port, was most attractive.

Kobe houses

We managed to organise an all day visit to Kyoto, the ancient capital of Japan.
Cherry blossom season is the best time to visit Japan and we were there bang on cue. Kyoto could be among the 'hundred places to visit before I die'. It has the most wonderful temples set alongside beautiful lakes,

gardens (Zen), and all within easy walking distance of one another. There were very few tourists and entry was free.

I remember an evening in Kobe. We had decided to go ashore and eat Japanese style. Studying the lurid coloured menus we struggled to find anything that appealed. At that time proper English people did not eat raw fish! One of the things we found were some sparrows barbecued whole, very tasty indeed. Meat was rarely on offer which probably explains why it is only recently that the Japanese have grown a bit taller. We settled for fish and chips.

From Kobe we sailed down through the Inland Sea to Sasebo. This had been the main United Nations support base during the Korean War which had only ended five years previously, so was quite familiar to some of our ship's company. However, it was yet another American base, and therefore not of great interest.

We returned to the Inland Sea to a little Japanese seaside town called Beppu. This was a delightful spot famous for its volcanic baths, which I didn't try. As usual not a soul spoke English. However the locals did put on a Japanese song and dance act for the ship's company. I've no idea what the sailors made of this but as Duty Officer I noted that several returned beaming in the early hours. Nobody could doubt that Beppu was the real Japan.

Mayoral reception at Beppu

Japanese garden and bathhouse, Beppu

Then we sailed to Nagoya which was a pretty big place even then. A very busy port but at last we were beginning to get the hang of things Japanese. We even ventured onto trains, not having the least idea where we were going. Getting onto the train was an extraordinary experience. You lined up alongside the train entrances marked on the platform, along with the rest of Japan. After the exiting passengers had come out you were lifted by the hordes into the train. Their heads were roughly level with your chest so you could gesticulate to your colleague who was some distance down the carriage. Of course the trains kept time to the nearest second. Somehow or another we managed to get back to Nagoya.

US Banana helicopter and Observation Post Mazie

Join the Navy, see the world?

So we bade farewell to Japan after a memorable cruise, and we set off for Inchon in Korea. From Inchon the Americans flew us up to the 28th Parallel in a banana helicopter, predecessor of the Chinook. Things were still very tense between North and South Korea. You could see the North Koreans trying to work out who these visitors to the U.N. demarcation line were.

The North/South Korean border – 28th Parallel

By now, after fourteen months away, we were ready to start on the passage home where the ship was to pay off into the Reserve Fleet. However we had a few adventures before that was achieved. Of course we couldn't go home without a final visit to Hong Kong for a few days. I did a last bit of shopping - I remember getting a camphorwood chest which has proved useful over the years for storing the collection of family photos. Shortly after arrival at Hong Kong, the girls from 'Jenny's Side Party' arrived on board. Every Royal Naval ship which visited Hong Kong was allocated a team of girls by Jenny Ah Soo. These charming, smiling girls essentially looked after the ship's side, washing and painting it very efficiently from sampans. The Navy supplied the paint and scrubbing materials, while Jenny and her girls made their living selling the sailors soft drinks, clothes and toys, waiting at cocktail parties and recycling 'gash' (rubbish).

Jenny had a very good relationship with the Staff of Commodore, Hong Kong so that she was prepared for a ship's visit, sometimes even before the ship itself knew it was going to Hong Kong. She was awarded the British Empire Medal in 1980 and died in 2010 aged 92. I often wonder what happened to the likes of Jenny after the British handed Hong Kong over to the Chinese in 1997.

Jenny's side party girls

Commissioning pennants have a mystique all of their own. Fundamentally you fly this white ribbon from the masthead on leaving your base for the last time. There is a formula for calculating the length of the pennant but that escapes me. It has to do with the length of time you have been in commission and the length of the vessel flying it. Anyway MODESTE had an extensive pennant on leaving Hong Kong. You need somebody at the stern to make sure it doesn't get wrapped around the propellers.

We had several matters to attend to before we were allowed to sail home. A short cruise round North Borneo to start with. We passed through the Mindoro Strait in the Philippines. This is an attractive passage but requires some very precise navigation. Our first stop in Borneo was Tawau, for the third time. Then we moved round the corner to Sandakan, famous for the export of a particular hardwood called lignum vitae used for propeller bearings. I found something much more interesting, in the form of the local Scottish mill owner's daughter. She took me out in a fast motor boat to a beautiful sandy beach where we were the only two people on it. Very nice!

Then we visited Kudat (Simpayang Mengayau), and some people went off to view a long house, home to a particularly bestial race of Borneo headhunters. Last stop Jesselton (Kota Kinabulu) where there was little except the Colonial Administration office for British North Borneo. I should have explained earlier that the southern part of the island of Borneo belongs to Indonesia.

We then had three weeks at Singapore maintaining the ship for its passage home. I spent most of the time staying at my father's house in Singapore, going to swim at the Tanglin Club or bargaining for Persian rugs which I couldn't afford.

On sailing from Singapore we received instructions to sail "with all despatch" (=17 knots) to the Persian Gulf, to protect British interests there, as the King of Iraq (King Feisal) had been deposed. Iraq was technically a British Protectorate after the dividing of Arab lands at the end of the First World War in 1921, the Balfour Agreement. Syria and Lebanon went to France. Iraq, Palestine, Egypt and the Sudan became British Protectorates. In 1958 the Shatt-el-Arab river, which divides Iraq and Iran, had the largest oil exporting terminal at its mouth, run by the Anglo-American Oil Company. So the Persian Gulf was critical to British interests. Ten days after leaving Singapore the mighty MODESTE arrived at Bahrain ready for whatever tasks were required. The biggest problem in the Persian Gulf was not the enemy, whomsoever that might have been, but the heat. The air temperature at the end of July 1958 was 40ºC in the middle of the day. The temperature in the boiler room was over 50ºC, so we had to get the stokers out for a lime juice every 30 minutes. They used to get really bad prickly heat.

Ammo replenishment in the Persian Gulf

We had two tasks: to search dhows for arms being smuggled from Iran to Iraq, and to let the local sheiks know that we meant business.

We anchored off Dubai, which was nothing more than a very smelly fishing port. The Captain and I dressed in full whites with swords and medals and went to call on Sheikh Abdullah, grandfather of the present (2009) Sheikh Mohammed bin Rashid Al Maktoum. His mud-walled palace was about five miles away out in the desert. On arrival we were ushered into his presence. We had a translator because the Sheikh spoke virtually no English. We were offered tea. He seemed pretty pleased to see us. This was long before oil started to gush there.

Searching an Arab dhow in Persian Gulf

A week spent searching dhows was pretty tedious to say the least. There were plenty of them but we didn't find anything. On 10th August we finally sailed from the Persian Gulf stopping at Aden, passing through the Suez Canal, and stopping at Malta on the way home.

After nearly 18 months away, we arrived at Portsmouth on 22nd September 1958 to a big welcome from family and friends. For all that time MODESTE had been almost my entire existence. This had been my first appointment as a proper Naval Officer, i.e. not under training. It is difficult to describe how involved in the life of a ship you can become. In the Far East we were operating from our own resources

Self on MODESTE's bridge

Ship's Company MODESTE

most of the time. So, providing you have a good mix of capable officers and sailors, you can develop a very special atmosphere. I can't remember a single unhappy occasion in MODESTE .

On return to Portsmouth I was ordered to prepare the ship for the Reserve Fleet which really involved encasing the whole ship in plastic sheeting, not a very invigorating pastime. However a small team of very competent sailors did the hard work, while I remained on the end of a telephone in London, available to come down to Portsmouth at short notice if needed. During this period I managed to meet my future bride, Rosemary Green, who, having recently graduated from Girton College, Cambridge, was doing a post-graduate secretarial course with a view to working abroad! Rosemary was described by my best man's flatmate as "nice girl but not your type".

Just before Christmas I signed MODESTE away. Not long after she was towed off to the scrap yard.

Chapter 10
HMS SURPRISE
January 1959 to September 1960
Lieutenant

To be appointed to the Commander-in-Chief Mediterranean's flagship was prestigious. HMS SURPRISE was described as a despatch vessel, why, I don't know, because her maximum speed was 17 knots. In fact her primary role was to ferry the Admiral on official visits around the Mediterranean, when she was not tethered to a buoy at Grand Harbour, Valetta, Malta.

HMS SURPRISE entering Venice

SURPRISE was originally a wartime Loch class frigate but her antisubmarine weapons aft had been removed and replaced by an extensive teak quarterdeck. Beneath the quarterdeck had been installed some very palatial cabins and reception rooms. So SURPRISE was considered by the rest of the Fleet as a floating cocktail party platform. That didn't bother me!

The previous but one Commander-in-Chief had been Lord Louis Mountbatten, so you can imagine that SURPRISE always had a high profile in Malta. During the Coronation Review at Spithead, SURPRISE was used by the Queen when she reviewed the Fleet, perhaps the ship's finest hour. Flying out to Malta was a sad occasion for me because I had proposed to my bride-to-be and we knew we were going to be apart for a few months. In those days a flight to Malta took the best part of a day because the turboprop aircraft had to refuel at a NATO airfield near Toulon.

HMS SURPRISE in Grand Harbour, Malta

Malta at that time was an excellent place to be based (and later on to live). The island has a very pleasant climate, with a very mild winter, and is populated by the Maltese who are a mix of the Italian and Arab races. Their language is more Arabic than Italian. In some ways they combine the best attributes of both Arab and Italian, though they could not be described as industrious. Their extraordinary courage was well demonstrated during World War II, the whole island being awarded the George Cross.

HMS SURPRISE leaves Grand Harbour, Malta

Because the island is so dry and rocky and therefore doesn't support much agriculture, many Maltese migrated to Australia after World War II. During the 1950's the main source of Malta's income was the Naval Dockyard and support to the three services. Tourism was little developed then which meant we could swim under the Mediterranean sun in little sheltered coves with hardly anyone there. We also used to go on the most marvellous boat picnics (banyans). The island was still a British colony and so a lot of the pomp and circumstance associated with status continued. Today it seems faintly ridiculous and perhaps it was not altogether surprising that the Maltese were soon to agitate for independence.

Ships in Sliema Creek, Malta

SURPRISE was not really a warship and was probably a bit of a nuisance in a proper naval exercise, so happily we weren't often asked to do anything very demanding. However we did make an effort on one occasion, perhaps to satisfy the civil servants in the Ministry of Defence? Our beautiful teak quarterdeck was covered in great sheets of steel so that we could carry two Westland helicopters – dirty, noisy, oily things. With these embarked, we set off for an amphibious exercise with the American Sixth Fleet. We assisted in landing US and UK marines on the Libyan coast. When the exercise was over we decided to have a cocktail party, our 'main armament'! The US Navy was invited and black velvets (Guinness and champagne) were served. Unfortunately one American Admiral had a few too many and had to be carried into his boat by "limey" (ie British) sailors, very undignified.

I forgot to mention that I did have some duties to perform on board. At sea I was the ship's communications officer, but I didn't have a lot to do when the Admiral's staff were embarked. One of only three qualified watch-keepers at sea kept me pretty busy. I was also responsible for catering for the ship's company, a pretty thankless task with the pitiful amount of money provided by the Admiralty for this purpose. I often overran the budget and was reprimanded for having done so. Ships with larger numbers of sailors on board had bigger budgets to play with. By way of riposte to my Captain, I pointed this out in writing in the correct service manner. He endorsed my letter when forwarding it on to the Commander-in-Chief. Shortly afterwards the victualling allowance for the whole Navy was substantially increased, though I doubt whether that was as a direct result of my representations.

Once again my eighteen months in the SURPRISE reads like a present day cruise brochure, the difference being the length of time we spent in places and that we were being paid for the pleasure, although not very much!

Early in my time on board we set off on a cruise round the northern and western Mediterranean. The Commander-in-Chief (C-in-C) Mediterranean was embarked, so first stop was Naples for discussions with C-in-C South, an American admiral commanding NATO forces. At that time Naples was a city of considerable poverty. The narrow winding streets leading up the hill not far from the port were full of people trying to sell their wares. As wardroom wine caterer, I managed to buy some 3 litre straw-covered bottles of Chianti 'en primeur' for the same price as a bottle of Coca Cola. Being new wine it was slightly fizzy and very refreshing and therefore easy to consume in large quantities. Chianti appears to have gone upmarket since then but has never tasted so good. Leather goods were fantastic value, a good opportunity to buy nice things for a future bride.

As a cultural expedition we managed to fit in a visit to Herculaneum, about 30 miles south of Naples. It is one of the Roman towns submerged by volcanic ash from Vesuvius. It has many incredible murals like Pompeii but is spread out over a larger area and therefore not so crowded. Quite definitely one of those "must see" places.

The next stop was La Spezia, a predominantly NATO port within easy reach of Rome. The Naval Attaché in Rome lent the ship his car, a large Humber. As the only European qualified driver on board I had virtually the sole use of this vehicle for our three-day stay. So we drove around the sights of Rome – Colosseum, St Peter's, Spanish Steps and so forth. In those days Italy was still recovering from the war so there was virtually no traffic, impossible to imagine today, but what an experience.

From La Spezia we went to Calvi in Corsica. We anchored off for a couple of days. Today it is a major tourist attraction but then, to walk round the castle and the narrow streets, much as they had been for hundreds of years, was a great joy. One could have the most superb seafood lunch for just a few shillings; even an impoverished Lieutenant could afford that.

Then we sailed over to Toulon, the French naval base. For the French, whisky has always been the aperitif of choice so we agreed to swap bottles of duty-free whisky for cases of burgundy, mostly Gevry Chambertin. Both sides seemed very happy with this arrangement, Scotch being pretty well unobtainable in France at that time. We were delighted to receive cases of burgundy at one shilling each. Their Lordships of the Admiralty's rules for auditing wine didn't cater for this situation, so we had to indulge in some "creative" accounting before the auditors would sign off my accounts. Relations with the French Navy at this period could sometimes be frosty, bearing in mind that we had despatched their Mediterranean fleet to the bottom of Oran harbour during the Second World War. Amazing how a few bottles of Scotch can improve matters.

Barcelona was an altogether different port of call, very much a place for sailors. We were always conscious that most of the places we visited were too expensive for most of the ship's company. The bars were fantastic, with brandy a penny a tot, and the cabaret shows were decidedly racy, with plenty of young ladies to entertain in their various ways.

By this time the Navy's standard aperitif (pink gin) had been replaced by the Horse's Neck (brandy and ginger ale). A Spanish brandy called Fundador goes remarkably well with Messrs Schweppes' ginger ale. So the Wine Caterer leapt into action once more and purchased several crates of Fundador to keep us going for a week or two.

On the way back from Barcelona to Malta the ship ran into a huge storm in the Gulf of Lyons. The Gulf of Lyons is relatively shallow, so if the wind blows strongly, short steep seas get up. So bad was this storm that the ship was obliged to steam at slow speed ahead into the sea for twenty-four hours, the only time this happened to me in twenty-eight years service in the Royal Navy, and in the Mediterranean at that.

That was our spring cruise. The summer cruise was very different. We sailed from Malta to Piraeus, the port for Athens, where we embarked the Greek Royal Family – King George, the Queen of Greece, Princesses Sophie and Irene, and Prince Constantine. Because of the Mountbatten family connection, the SURPRISE had often substituted for the Greek Royal Yacht which they didn't have. The Admiral didn't come because his quarters were required for the royal personages, so SURPRISE's officers provided escort services when required.

We anchored off the most perfect beach on the island of Skiathos, in those days a small white-housed town in the distance, and not a soul in sight. The King and Queen paid official visits to the town while we entertained the Prince and Princesses to a picnic lunch. Then overnight to Santorini. It took us a long time to find somewhere in the lagoon shallow enough to anchor. The island of Santorini was formed by probably the biggest earthquake the Mediterranean has ever experienced, at least in recent times. Santorini didn't exist until this earthquake in 1600 BC when it arose out of the sea. The subsequent tsunami submerged many of the Minoan settlements on Crete 90 miles away and the Greco-roman city of Alexandria in Egypt several hundred miles away. It was my turn to be on anchor watch so I never had the chance to take the obligatory donkey ride several hundred feet up the hill to the town.

The Corinth canal was originally conceived in early Greek times to obviate the need to sail round the Corinth peninsula but was not available to shipping use until the 1890's. It was damaged by the Germans during their occupation of Greece during the Second World War but was re-opened in the late 1940's. With the Greek Royal family aboard we had no difficulty in gaining permission to go through. It didn't look like it, but there was plenty of room for a ship of SURPRISE's size.

The next day we moored at the small port of Eta and were taken by car to visit Delphi, the site of the Oracle. We were the only visitors but we did have an excellent guide who explained the purpose of the main buildings. Next stop was Corfu where the Greek Royal Family disembarked. They had a summer palace complete with goose-stepping sentries, a practice the Mountbatten family seem to carry out at all their palaces (e.g. Copenhagen).

Before they disembarked we had a farewell party on board. We turned part of the apartments aft into a disco for about a dozen of the young. I spent a lot of time dancing with Princess Sophie who explained to me the very claustrophobic existence they lived on mainland Greece. They weren't really very popular, not being, or speaking, Greek. They were later exiled by the "Colonels". Sophie became Queen of Spain and I often think of my charming partner when I see her on the television.

After all that royal excitement, there was a trip "round the corner" to Istanbul. It was/is one of the great places to visit with its extraordinary mix of Islamic and Christian buildings and cultures. And who can resist a session bargaining for a carpet in the bazaar? That was my first essay into the world of carpet purchasing, something I've much enjoyed over the years. We didn't find time to take the ferry across to Asia nor a trip to Gallipoli. I definitely feel that the Blue Mosque was much bluer in those days, there were certainly fewer people.

From Istanbul we paid a visit to Haifa, Israel's main port. Remember that ten years before Israel had achieved independence by their terrorists (Irgun) gunning down British 'occupying' soldiers. Somehow or another the Jewish race have always made me feel uncomfortable. I can't say that I enjoyed this visit to their very busy seaport. Although we didn't get up to Jerusalem, we did visit a kibbutz not far from the Golan Heights. The kibbutz was full of young people from just about every nation under the sun, holidaying there was a very popular student pastime.

Back to Malta to recover from all that cruising. In fact, not for long because we quickly set off for the Med Fleet regatta at Augusta, Sicily. This involved rowing in whalers against other ships in the Fleet. We barely had enough officers to make up the crew of five plus coxswain. Some ships had trained for months for this so we were at a big disadvantage. Also we had been too busy cruising to keep fit. Excuses!

Rosemary, bride-to-be, managed to hitch a lift in one of the spectator boats, so we did slip away for a couple of nights at Taormina; everything was pretty affordable in those days.

This is perhaps the moment to describe something of the life ashore in Malta. Rosemary rented a small, very Maltese stone flat at Sliema, a couple of miles from Grand Harbour, which she shared with a girlfriend.

There was a well known officer's bar called the City Gem at the bottom of the road, very convenient! She managed to find a job, part teaching and part secretarial, at the Naval School, which helped to augment the rather meagre funds. The climate is extremely good, so plenty of sport was available – polo (not me), swimming, rugby, hockey, sailing. Malta has many archaeological sites, catholic churches and Knights Templar fortresses. It has been occupied at some time or other by Phoenicians, Turks, Knights Templar, Romans, Greeks, British etc. All of them left their mark in some form or another, so Malta is a great place to explore. The rougher forms of night entertainment were plentiful – bars and ladies of the night –especially in Straight Street, Valetta (known as "the Gut"). For the more sophisticated, plenty of Wardroom and private parties. Strangely enough good eating places were few and far between and inordinately expensive. The Maltese were never famed for their cuisine, very stodgy pasta being the norm.

A few of us were lent a beautiful flat owned by a South African lady. We decided to throw a party (as one does) and mixed a fruit punch (consisting essentially of the Maltese wine Marsovin) in the bath. Great party, until next morning when we came to clear up. The remains of the punch had stripped the enamel off the bath. So replacement needed i.e. very expensive party. Amazing the resilience of the human stomach.

At that time, just across the water from Malta, Libya was ruled by an Arab sheikh called King Idris (there used to be an orange drink of that name!). His palace was to the east of that huge country. His capital town was at Tripoli in the west, several hundred miles distant. So each year SURPRISE used to embark this very smelly old man at Benghazi and take him to visit his subjects at Tripoli. After its tribulations during World War II, Tripoli was a pretty run down place, so we didn't spend much time in the town. Instead we went down the coast to visit Leptis Magna, the nearly complete ruins of a Roman seaport, a truly wonderful experience. As usual we were the only visitors.

For some reason or other the British Ambassador to Greece needed to visit Crete. Difficult to do without your normal Rolls Royce, and a ship to host suitable parties. Said vehicle duly arrived in Malta and was lifted onto SURPRISE's quarterdeck and off we went to Crete. Because there was no crane at Heraklion the Rolls Royce had to be offloaded at the far end of the island. I was then invited to drive this superb machine most of the length of the island back to Heraklion. There was only one road and it was a night-time trip passing through unlit villages. Goats and children seemed to be all over the narrow mountainous road. That was frankly one of the hairiest drives I've ever undertaken. A much relieved D.A. arrived at Heraklion in the early hours of the morning with an intact Rolls Royce.

The next day we were taken on a full day tour of Knossos, the Minoan town which was still being excavated. We were very privileged to have the head archaeologist conduct us round. The degree of civilisation they achieved in 400BC was astounding, even if some of their religious beliefs were a bit bizarre. Knossos was high enough up not to be affected by the tsunami mentioned earlier.

In December 1959, SURPRISE went into refit at Malta which gave Rosemary and myself the moment we had been waiting for to get married. We flew home for a couple of weeks and, on a very cold January day, were married in Salisbury Cathedral with an impressive guard of honour to greet us outside. Three days of honeymoon in the New Forest had to suffice before returning to duty.

Wedding, 9th January 1960

Once the ship had been restored to its normal pristine condition after refit, SURPRISE paid a visit to Venice. The Maltese have highly decorated rowing boats called dghaisas. Each ship in Malta was allocated one, complete with oarsman. They were normally used to take the ship's company to and from the shore. We were very proud of ours and decided to take it to Venice. We thought it might make the Venetian gondolas look rather tatty and it did, to the point where the gondoliers threatened our poor oarsman with violence, so we hoisted the dghaisa inboard to avoid further trouble. Italians!?

A Maltese dghaisa

Venice was a great place to visit. There were very few tourists and things were relatively cheap. We organised a visit to the Murano glass factory where I bought a lovely green glass bowl. Unfortunately it didn't survive the trip back to the UK.

On 19 February 1960, Rosemary's 24th birthday, we were invited to a party aboard BASTION, a landing craft tank (LCT), anchored in Grand Harbour. During the evening the announcement came to "splice the mainbrace". The Queen had given birth to Prince Andrew.

Some time later, we were told that it was time for us to earn our keep for a week or two. There was a major uprising taking place on the island of Cyprus. Greek Cypriot terrorists, under the name of EOKA, were regularly ambushing Army and RAF units on the island, and were terrorising the Turkish Cypriots. So the Royal Navy steamed round Cyprus at night endeavouring to catch arms smugglers. SURPRISE was as suited as any ship to this activity, which lasted for ten days or so. Rosemary hitched a lift in our accompanying oiler and so we squeezed a couple of days ashore visiting Kyrenia and Famagusta.

On return to Malta I learnt that I was appointed to the Dartmouth Training Squadron, the end of a fantastic eighteen months. Malta was a great place to start one's married life and, with so many happy memories, is often re-visited.

Chapter 11
HMS ACUTE
October 1960 to October 1961
Lieutenant

After 18 months in the sunny Mediterranean it was time for a job in the working Navy. HMS ACUTE was an Algerine minesweeper based at Dartmouth, and I was the Navigating Officer responsible for getting this little ship in and out of Dartmouth's very congested harbour and for teaching Cadets the elementary rudiments of coastal navigation. Now that was never a very strong suit of mine (as many friends will know), but somehow or other we got through 12 months without running aground or hitting anything, the first time this had been achieved in the Dartmouth Training Squadron.

The most notable event during this appointment was the arrival of first child and son, Timothy, in Salisbury on the Queen's 'real' birthday, 21st April 1961. We were lucky enough to have his christening on board ACUTE, making use of the ship's bell in the traditional naval way.

The seagoing motion of an Algerine minesweeper was truly unpleasant and many cadets must have had very unhappy memories of their time in ACUTE. Trying to instruct seasick Cadets in a confined space was not a very jolly task and often not very successful. Coastal navigation was part radar, part visual, but inevitably very repetitive as we went in and out of Dartmouth each day.

We had a cruise to Norway to break up the monotony. The North Sea was incredibly rough. Very sadly we lost a Petty Officer overboard – nobody saw it happen – and the body was never recovered. He had been having marital problems so presumably this was his way of ending them.

The Chaplain of the Royal Naval College officiated at son Timothy's christening, July 1961

We visited Bergen and Tromso which was very pleasant in mid-summer. Rosemary and I had a very happy domestic year with our first son Timothy. We took a cottage in a small Devon village called Capton. One side of the cottage was hillside and it was therefore incredibly damp. There was no mains gas or electricity but plenty of running water! A very Devonian Devon family lived next door. Apart from assisting my efforts in creating a garden they brewed truly lethal parsnip wine that produced a headache like no other!

We were able to take part in some of the Naval College's wardroom activities. I remember tearing my mess undress uniform playing bar billiards with three officers who all went on to become Admirals, but not because of their prowess at bar billiards. A very expensive Mess dinner!

At this time Cadets entered the Naval College at the age of eighteen or thereabouts, their number was supplemented by a few Upper Yardmen. They were ratings under training to become officers. Cadets totalled several hundred as the Navy still had a sizable fleet, and some cadets were going into the Fleet Air Arm and Submarine Service. Instruction was entirely Naval oriented, and they only spent one year at the College. It was very refreshing to be teaching young men with un-bounding enthusiasm.

We managed to fit in a trip to St Malo in Brittany in between our training duties in ACUTE. Now that is the original navigator's challenge. The tidal range at St Malo at spring tides is up to 45 feet. We locked into the basin at the top of the tide. Returning from a very excellent platter

HMS ACUTE, 20-24 July 1961, Amsterdam

of 'fruits de mer', I looked over the dockside wall to see where we had entered and there was nothing but mud and rocks. Very scary!

We were also allowed a half-term break to go over and visit Amsterdam for four days. I of course concentrated on the cultural aspects of the visit – beer and cheese. Actually all I can remember is that it rained the whole time we were there, in July.

During the winter we were based in Plymouth so I had to drive back and forth to Dartmouth every day, a very hairy trip down icy, narrow Devon lanes.

In August 1961 their Lordships announced that ACUTE and sister ship JEWEL were to be retired and converted into razor blades. So we left Dartmouth for the last time with commissioning pennants flying.

HMS ACUTE and JEWEL leave Dartmouth for the last time

Chapter 12
Interpreter's Course, Paris
October 1961 to March 1962
Lieutenant

My appointing officer rang up and gave me a choice of two jobs, to become a shallow water diver or to do a French interpreter's course in Paris. The thought of crawling round the mud of Portsmouth Harbour in mid-winter didn't appeal one little bit, so I chose the French option, one of the best decisions I ever made, as it turned out.

We motored over to France with a few possessions and installed ourselves in a small flat near Porte de Saint Cloud on the edge of Paris. In the mornings I had a two-hour lesson with a formidable French lady, who had taught Admiral Mountbatten French. He apparently was a star pupil and I certainly wasn't! She had survived Paris under the Germans and didn't have a very high opinion of the 'Boche', a frequent subject for discussion during lessons. Trying to study in the afternoon with a baby who insisted on screaming the place down was not easy but Rosemary very gallantly took him to the park even in the middle of a very cold Paris winter.

This was a very interesting period to be living in Paris. President de Gaulle was still the idol of half the populace; equally loathed by the Socialist other half. His television speeches took place on about a monthly basis. Delivered in a slow, faultless French they were wonderful listening and reading material for students of French. In retrospect his blocking of Britain joining the Common Market probably was the right decision from Britain's point of view. We were not ready to be dominated by a Europe led by De Gaulle who had been so tiresome during World War II.

In 1960 De Gaulle granted independence to Algeria causing great consternation for the more than one million French citizens who lived there. They returned to France where there were few jobs, and a small number became OAS terrorists. Plenty of bombs went off in Paris but none near us.

Paris was a wonderful place to live, it still is. We didn't do much eating out but had several outings to the country at weekends. Food bought at the Sunday market in Saint Cloud was superb, and seemed quite reasonable. I found a nearby bar where I could get a dozen oysters and a glass of white wine before setting off for my French lesson. The other bar occupants had their usual breakfast – coffee and brandy – before setting off to work, the normal labourer's practice in France.

After three months, at the end of the Local Overseas Allowance period, I was obliged to send the family back to Salisbury. I moved "en famille" with the mother of a friend and her two children. My colloquial French improved no end. My landlady was a widow who worked, so the daytime was pretty cheerless but gave me time to swat for my Interpreter's exam. I took this in London in March. My tutor said: "Drink your usual half litre of red wine before the exam and you'll be fine". I had a very technical translation about nuclear reactors that I happened to have read about in the Figaro newspaper a few weeks previously, so all turned out well. While in the Navy I only used my limited interpreter skills twice, but, much later on, my knowledge of French did enable me to secure the best job ever, running British Telecom's office in Paris.

Reflecting on my six months in Paris, I gained a liking for the French way of life and language which remains with me to this day.

Chapter 13
HMS TIGER
April 1962 to April 1963
Lieutenant

After six months learning French in Paris, it was all a bit of a shock to go to sea in a major warship. TIGER was a 6-inch gun cruiser with the most modern fire control system afloat at that time, but none of that was of great interest to me as I was the ship's assistant navigator. In fact I did very little navigation as I was often being sent ahead to organise Fleet visits, which was a lot more fun. More about that anon.

It was pretty grim leaving Devonport and wife and small son for the Far East on a wet day in April knowing I was going to be away for a year and that it was unlikely the family would be able to join me during that time. The only consolation was that TIGER was a very happy ship full of lots of compatible 'spirits'.

In fact I joined at the mid-point in a two-year commission; time away was rather longer in those days. We stopped at Gibraltar for a couple of days before steaming on to the Suez Canal, the fourth transit for this hardy mariner! As the Assistant Navigator, I had to take control of the ship's handling, known as the 'con', for quite a bit of the passage, paying not very much attention to what the Egyptian canal pilot was saying. Six years previously (Suez Campaign) he had been in the Egyptian Navy, our enemy at that time! He seemed very friendly and not likely to try and run TIGER aground.

Just before Suez we changed into the white uniform that remained the 'rig of the day' for the next ten months. The sun shone and I assumed my normal feeling of happiness in warm climes.

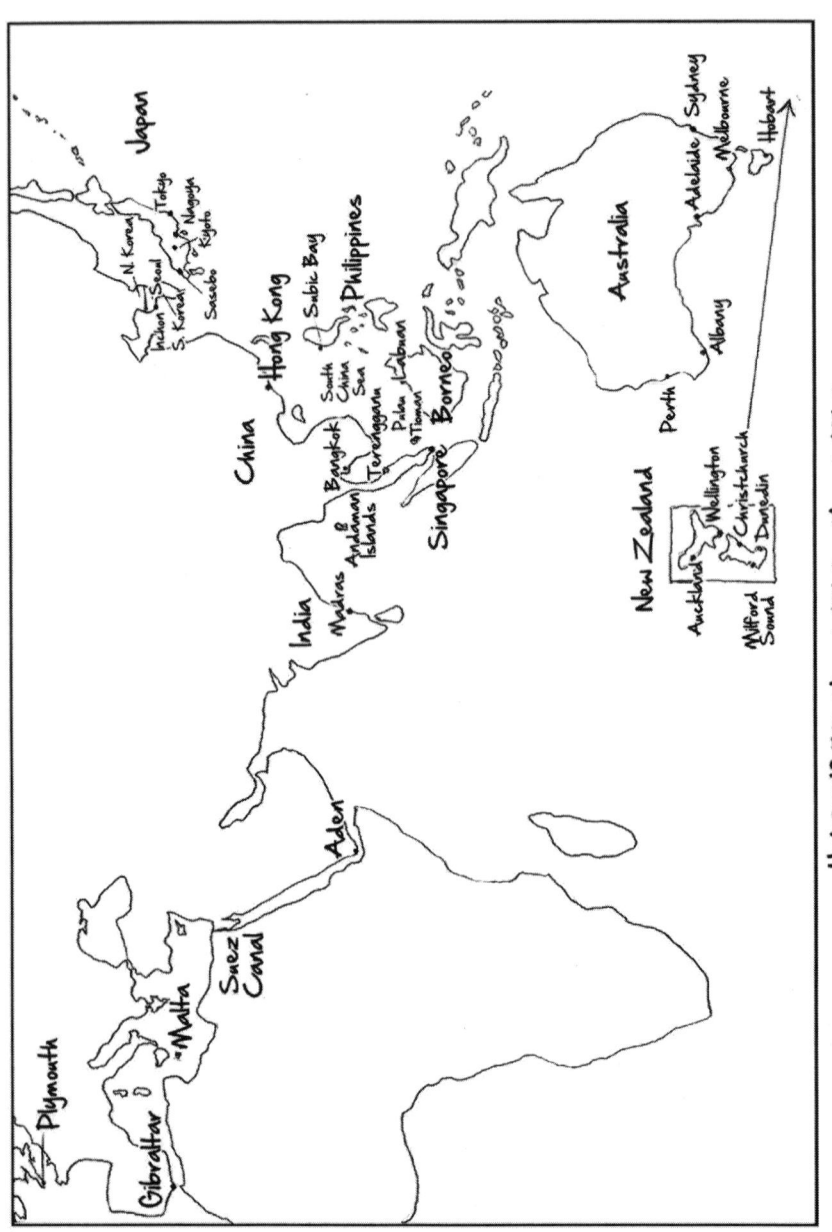

Map of HMS TIGER's route, March 1962-3

Even in April the Red Sea was grilling hot and none more so than the arid port of Aden. Aden was a duty-free port, and probably, with a bit of bargaining, the cheapest shopping anywhere. At any rate, I acquired a genuine Omega Seamaster watch that survives to this day. Aden was still a British protectorate and relatively peaceful. There was no evidence of riots or trouble with tribesmen up country in the Yemen.

Then it was a long trudge across the Arabian Sea, the Indian Ocean and then down the Malacca Straits to the Singapore Naval Base. We followed the normal practice of working tropical routine, 0700 to 1300, very pleasant. This left the afternoon free for sports and swimming followed, perhaps, by a few Singapore Sling cocktails (see below) at the Officer's Club, or a taxi ride to Singapore town. During the three weeks we had alongside at Singapore I tried to exercise every day – golf, tennis, hockey, rugby to name a few. It wasn't too bad a life.

A description of the island of Singapore in 1962 at the end of colonial rule might be informative. Singapore is a diamond-shaped island about the size of the Isle of Wight. The town is situated in the southwest part, whereas the bridge across to Johore Bahru in Malaysia and the Naval Base are in the northeast. The large naval base was therefore some twenty miles from the main shopping area, although there were a few stalls outside the main gate.

Singapore was administered by a High Commissioner and a substantial Foreign Office staff. There were three main ethnic groups on the island. The Chinese ran the majority of commercial activities as they normally do. The Malays provided the colour with their dress and ceremonies. The Indians tended to run the shops. The Singapore newspapers were beginning to report the activities of various ethnic leaders, the most prominent being Lee Kuan Yew who later became the all powerful leader of an independent Singapore and founder of today's modern state.

The town of Singapore was an hour's taxi ride from the Naval Base so a visit was not an everyday occurrence. Officers were members of the civilian Tanglin Club, an all-white preserve, good steaks, a swimming pool and a few unattached white girls. Other delights were bargaining at the shops for Persian carpets one could not possibly afford, watching Chinese girls 'taxi-dancing', a curious sort of cha-cha which avoided any form of body contact, while sipping a glass of Tiger beer, or having an alfresco supper at the food stalls in Chinatown for the princely sum of 50p. The expats and the wealthy Chinese definitely had the best of life in Singapore. There was a great deal of poverty in several parts of the island, particularly the port areas. Sailors used to prime themselves with large quantities of Tiger beer and then head for Boogie Street, infamous for its Katemites, lads who used to dress up in very fetching lady's clothing. Big disappointment there then!

Downtown Singapore was dominated by the Padang (village green) with its attendant cathedral and Raffles Hotel. A Singapore Sling at the Long Bar was still affordable in those days. This is my favourite recipe for a Singapore Sling: two measures gin, one of cherry brandy, a dash of Cointreau, lemon juice and Angostura bitters. Top the glass up with soda. There were a few proper shops in the Orchard Road. CK Tang's Chinese Emporium was very oriental and different.

One of my memories of my time in TIGER was the truly dreadful cabins for the junior officers. They were situated next to the main boiler-room bulkhead (wall). At sea the temperature was often over 40ºC and there was no air conditioning. So when one went on watch to the bridge for the middle watch (0001 to 0400) after no sleep, keeping awake was a real struggle.

HMS TIGER in Johore Straits

After a very leisurely spell in Singapore it was time to 'play sailors' once more. We gave the guns a good workout, including a shore bombardment against the idyllic tropical island of Pulau Tioman. There were a few natives living on the island but that didn't seem to matter. Apparently if a warship came into view they scarpered! It is strange to think that today Pulau Tioman has several five star hotels and is a great 'get away from it all' holiday spot.

On that particular visit my memory is of one incident only. I was Officer of the Watch in the afternoon on the Quarterdeck of TIGER and boats were taking the Ship's Company to and from the beach. A 32-foot motor boat was lying alongside the port gangway. I was just about to send it inshore when I noticed a grey shape under the boat. Its tail stuck out at the stern and its head at the bows. I pointed this out to the Leading Seaman who was coxing the boat. He turned a very obvious shade of grey. I remembered stories of how many survivors were attacked by this shark's ancestors when the PRINCE OF WALES and the REPULSE were sunk by the Japanese in 1941 not far from there. Needless to say we decided that swimming had better be suspended for the day.

After Pulau Tioman, it was across the South China Sea to Hong Kong. Over the years this place was almost my home port, but this time my stay was cut short. The Commander of TIGER was a great friend. I had served with him before and was to again. He despatched me by air to Seoul, the Korean capital, to organise the forthcoming Fleet visit to Inchon, Korea's main port.

Consequently I had a week staying at the British Embassy in Seoul, complete with US Navy car and driver. I had three tasks: organise the Admiral's programme, arrange for transport to get the Ship's company up to Seoul (a very rough, 50-mile drive), and outings and sports for the ship's companies – there were seven visiting ships in the Fleet. The American services were very generous and did all the hard work for me. In 1962 Korea was still recovering from the Korean War that had ended six years previously. The Americans were present in force and were virtually running the country. They were building hospitals, schools and roads. The Korean national dish is kimshi, a sort of pickled cabbage with garlic. This lingers on the breath "something horrible", so close contact is not advised. The country was primitive in the extreme; it is amazing how it has become an industrial power house in such a short space of time.

The First Secretary at the Embassy, a very cultured diplomat who went on to great things in the Foreign Office, took me under his wing. We visited such fabulous buildings in Seoul as the 1,000-year wooden and multi-coloured temple. Sadly this was burnt down in riots not so long ago.

Vandals were busy excavating many of the Korean grave sites and the results of their labours were to be found in the antique shops down the back alleys of Seoul. Pretty short of cash the best that I could manage was a small Tang vase of no great beauty. One of the wealthier officers acquired some celadon vases that I much admired.

North Korean/American Conference on the 28th Parallel

The US Army provided a helicopter to take us up to the 28th Parallel, the border between North and South Korea. At that time daily conferences between the two countries were held to discuss 'incidents'. We provided the material for that day because 'foreigners' were not theoretically allowed up to the border. It was a particularly eerie atmosphere with both sides glowering at each other across no-mans-land. I imagine it is much the same 47 years later.

So on to Japan. The Ship's Company were looking forward to this after a pretty dull time in Korea. We crossed the Inland Sea overnight. I think that was one of the most frightening middle watches I've ever experienced. To get to the Japanese Naval Academy on time we had to do 21 knots up the narrow, buoyed channel, and the visibility was about 50 yards. The Midshipman of the Watch and I did 15 minutes each glued to the radar screen. There were Japanese ferries crossing at similar speeds to ours. At about 0200 in the morning the Commander appeared on the bridge saying that a channel buoy had just scraped down the starboard side. I apologized and explained how difficult it was to stay in the Channel at the same time as avoiding crossing ships. At that moment I was just breathing a sigh of relief that we had missed a huge ferry that had passed 20 yards astern, which luckily the Commander hadn't seen.

The Japanese Naval College was modelled on Dartmouth, and had been completely re-built after the Second World War. The Royal Navy was much respected although all the training ships were of American origin. The next day we sailed up the Sumida River and berthed in the middle of Tokyo quite close to the main shopping district of Ginza. In the five years since my last visit things had become incredibly expensive. However it is always fun to walk round a Japanese department store people watching and viewing the not very useful stuff on sale. I took part in a visit to the Noritake china factory which was fascinating, hundreds of pretty, little Japanese girls sticking transfers onto plates.

We sailed overnight to the big commercial port of Nagoya, a much lower key place than Tokyo. The shops were full of mechanical toys, very good for 'grown up children', but my one child was really too small for such things.

Several of us managed to arrange a day visit to Kyoto. The beautiful temples and gardens and very old wooden houses are really something to behold and were just as I remembered. There were still very few tourists; it was very peaceful for Zen-style contemplation. The locals mostly wore traditional dress, such as kimonos, whereas suits were already the norm in the big cities.

Compared with the country I visited five years previously, the farmers continued to work the paddy fields without the assistance of much machinery. In contrast the cities were crammed with very ordinary little cars made by Nissan, Toyota et al. The Japanese motor industry was in its infancy and quality control was not their strongpoint. Jap cars were universally despised except by the Japanese of course! On the other hand they were producing the most sensational electronic equipment, such as Technics HiFi's. They were cheaper to buy in Hong Kong than in Japan. The extraordinary thing was no one in Japan spoke English, except for schoolchildren who kept repeating "Englishman is gentleman" - very good news - presumably they were taught this at school, although with what purpose I'm not sure. Japanese food is nowadays understood in Europe, but brightly coloured, raw fish was not very usual then. Fish in batter – tempura – was, on the other hand, delicious. Meat, except whale, was not much in evidence.

After Nagoya we sailed to the big American Navy Base at Sasebo. The British fleet had been based there during the Korean conflict. The Americans laid on a lot of entertainment for the Ship's Company but I can't remember anything about Sasebo - it was that memorable!

HMS TIGER refuelling with USS MANATEE

On the way back to Singapore, TIGER carried out exercises with the US Seventh Fleet, at that time the largest fleet in the world, based in the Philippines. After a few days in Singapore we embarked a party from the Greenjacket Regiment and the Royal Marines. We took them up the east coast of Malaysia to land them at Trengganu for an exercise in the jungle. This was to prove a useful trial for the real thing later on.

Cruisers like TIGER are not well suited to transporting soldiers because there is virtually no spare sleeping accommodation, so they slept on the upper deck, which was fine except during tropical downpours.

Photo: HMS TIGER in dry dock

TIGER had a couple of weeks in dry dock in Singapore to change a propeller. At one time this was the largest dry dock in the world so TIGER didn't fill much of it. We enjoyed this period because we went to live in the shore establishment (HMS TERROR) which was very comfortable and much cooler.

Our next trip was to Bangkok, in those days not so much of the tourist Mecca it is today. Perhaps it is the ideal mariner's port of call – oriental charms, cheap beer, fantastic photo opportunities and an exciting night life – in short plenty of scope for getting into trouble!

For those more culturally inclined, the profusion of golden temples and palaces was a delight. Have you noticed that in colour photos gold never seems to come out properly, or didn't in those days? I think we still have some Thai silk from this visit waiting to be made into cushion covers!

The Flag Lieutenant was unwell so, for three weeks, I was appointed in his place, an interesting experience working for a very demanding Admiral. From him I learnt at least one useful habit. If you made a mess of some task he didn't hesitate to tell you. But if he was pleased with your efforts he would send for you and say: "I thought you did that very well. Thank you." Just that. This leadership practice works well in military and civilian life I've found.

On 28th September 1962 the TIGER cruiser (or should that be "cruise ship"?!) set off for an extensive tour of Australia and New Zealand. The passage from Singapore to Sydney took several days, passing by many Indonesian islands including a small active volcano which typified how unsettled geologically that part of the world is.

Sydney Harbour

An eleven-day visit to Sydney was a great treat, even for those who had been there before. A comment from a member of TIGER's ship's company:

"Differences between the Australians and ourselves were interesting for this was my first visit to a country which we might expect to be like the UK. Although it is impossible to generalise, for there are so many different types of Australian originating from many countries, in the main they are more straightforward, friendly and blunt than us. They were wonderful hosts. The new words such as sport, sheila, dinkum, cobber and Pommie rapidly became second nature".

The contrasts between the good life in sunny Australia and that experienced by the average Royal Navy matelot were marked, to the point where a few, with some assistance from their Australian girlfriends, chose to leave (or desert) on a permanent basis. During my long stay in Perth later on, this was to be a problem.

My visit to Sydney was enlivened by the arrival of my brother for a few days. I hadn't seen him for five years in which time he had become a typical Aussie. As he was a poor university student, I had to fund his activities.

So we sailed across the Tasman Sea to Auckland, New Zealand's largest city. After Sydney it was decidedly low key but a good place from which to visit the hot springs at Rotorua or go fishing on Lake Taupo.

I remember Auckland most for my last game of rugby. The TIGER XV played a New Zealand Navy side, yours truly a prop forward as usual. Shortly after half-time I ran into an enormous Maori forward and changed direction 180 degrees. I have no recollection of the second half but was told I played as badly as normal. However I decided after the game that that was a good moment to throw away my rugby boots, I was still only 27 years old.

New Zealand was then a throwback to pre-Second World War times in the UK. The airline pilots used to announce before arriving in Auckland: "Put your clocks back 45 years as you are about to land in New Zealand". It wasn't quite as bad as that, but the population was only three million, of which a quarter were Maori or Islanders from the South Pacific. New Zealanders were mostly farmers and of course depended heavily on exporting their produce to the UK. Living in isolation the people tended to be very hospitable but a bit dull. It was to be many years before Auckland became a bustling city with the publicity

Wellington Harbour

from the America's Cup. It is a great country to visit as a tourist with some of the best scenery and wine but you might not want to live there permanently.

Next we sailed down the North Island coast to Wellington, the capital of New Zealand. Wellington, situated in the Cook Strait which separates the North and South Islands, has a reputation for being windy and experiencing earthquakes and tremors, quite a good place for your capital city you might think. However, happily, we didn't experience either.

Our accompanying frigate, the LOCH KILLISPORT, was commanded by a Fleet Air Arm Captain, a well-known playboy. He hired the only night club in Wellington for an evening. By ten o'clock we had consumed the club's stock of champagne, so he imported the contents of his cellar from his ship and by 2am that too was gone. I have to say that it was a very good party.

While in Sydney, TIGER's Captain, whose brother was the racing correspondent for the Daily Telegraph, took us to the races at Randwick. So as mentor we had someone who really could pick the best of the horseflesh. Racing in Australia and New Zealand was organised so that you had a two-week race meeting at each of Sydney, Wellington, Melbourne and Adelaide in that order. Many of the same horses ran at all four meetings. Having tried our hand at Randwick, the Captain and the usual four of us were invited to the owners' boxes at Wellington. The owners were only too pleased to 'suggest' the possible winners. I had six winners in seven races at Wellington which paid for my entire Australian and New Zealand cruise! That's what I call hospitality.

After Wellington we sailed to Lyttleton in the South Island, which is the port for Christchurch. To get there you had to steam quite a long way up a channel past the most beautiful hills. At Christchurch I managed to spend a couple of days on a sheep station in the midst of the shearing season. Twenty sheep an hour, but you need to average that if you have several thousand to shear. The station I stayed at was one of several owned by that farmer. He was a very nice man but rather taciturn; I suppose that comes from living such a solitary and sheep-oriented existence.

Dunedin, our next port of call, is often considered to be more Scottish than most places in Scotland. True to form we arrived in a drizzle, with the ship's tame bagpiper playing standing on the forward gun turret. The ship berthed in the middle of the town. To make us feel welcome the locals had waived their normal licensing laws – pubs normally shut at 6pm and all day Sunday. A deer-stalking expedition was organised and it was alleged that 102 deer were shot – they had become a plague for farmers and gardeners. Venison seemed to appear very frequently on the menus thereafter.

TIGER's final visit in New Zealand was to Milford Sound. This is a fjord on the south west coast best visited from the sea, every bit as spectacular as any of the Norwegian fjords I have visited, with towering rock faces and lots of birds and seals. As Navigator for the day I had to pay attention but it wasn't really very difficult as the rock faces were sheer with two or three kilometres of water under the keel.

On leaving Milford Sound we set course for Hobart in Tasmania. The Tasman Sea was in a very angry mood, so the ship was pretty scruffy for arrival at Hobart. Without royal distractions this time, the locals were very hospitable to many members of TIGER's ship's company. Pommie sailors were something of a novelty to 'Tassie' girls.

HMS TIGER in Milford Sound

HMS TIGER in Milford Sound

HMS TIGER in Milford Sound

On arrival at Melbourne, two days after Hobart, I was told that I was to be the Fleet Liaison Officer at Perth, Western Australia to prepare for the Fleet visit in conjunction with the 1962 Commonwealth Games so I had to pack my bags and fly to Perth. However I just managed to fit in an attendance at Flemington Races for the Melbourne Cup. In spite of our New Zealand knowledge I only managed to back four winners this time, but that included the winner of the Cup. It was all a bit like Derby Day with sun! The Aussie women were distinctly overdressed but easy on the eye nevertheless.

At Perth I was met by a term mate from Training Cruiser days, and was given an Australian Navy Holden car for my use for three weeks, so had the necessary facilities to carry out a demanding assignment. The first requirement was to ensure that an aircraft carrier (ARK ROYAL), a cruiser (TIGER), two Royal Navy destroyers, two Australian Navy destroyers, and one New Zealand frigate could all be fitted into Fremantle harbour. There were already three passenger liners in, being used as visitor accommodation. I calculated that the ARK ROYAL had six inches under the keel where she was due to berth. As the bottom was mud I reckoned that the ARK would slice through it if necessary. After a few nail-biting moments (on my part) she berthed without difficulty.

My second responsibility was to organise plenty of entertainment for the sailors – dances, trips to the trotting races, visits to properties (farms), sport of every sort, beach parties – there were only 6,800 sailors to be catered for.

My third task was to co-ordinate my Admiral's programme and seating. The Games were opened by the Duke of Edinburgh, so I had to ensure that the Admiral attended the Opening Ceremony but in most other respects he steered clear of the Duke's schedule. The one person who never saw anything of the Games was yours truly who couldn't fit it into my busy programme!

HMS TIGER at Albany

Each evening before her arrival, I had to signal TIGER with an update of all the programmes. Two days before TIGER arrived I was ordered down to Albany, 350 miles to the south of Perth, where TIGER was at anchor. My Aussie colleague and I took turns driving. I went out by boat and spent 30 minutes briefing the Admiral and the ship's staff on their programmes, and then drove 350 miles back to Perth. It was twenty years before the arrival of mobile phones.

One of my main concerns was the number of deserters we might expect from the visiting ships, particularly the ARK ROYAL. The local Royal Australian Navy shore establishment already had 13 sailors locked up from a recent Royal Navy visit. Australia with a great climate, virtually full employment and a very relaxed lifestyle was superficially an attractive alternative to what was experienced on the lower deck. It was comparatively easy to hitch a lift into the outback, but very few stayed when they discovered what a tough life that really was. When we left Perth we had 200 missing. As I sailed with the fleet, they became someone else's problem. The normal penalty for desertion was two years in a military prison.

London Court, Perth WA

Track event at the 1962 Commonwealth Games

At the time of the 1962 Commonwealth Games, Perth, and its port of Fremantle, only had a population of 400,000. They coped remarkably well with an influx of 30,000 visitors. Adverts were run in the local newspaper: "Show our visitors your sunny WA smile", which inevitably led to a bit of mickey-taking. One enterprising company was so proud of the local environment that they were selling canned Perth air, principally for the visitors to take home. They couldn't take home the "sunny WA smiles".

It had been an enormous privilege to be asked to organise this visit, and my Admiral thanked me for my efforts.

We were looking forward to a relaxing trip back to Singapore. That was not to be. On 6th December I was summoned to the wireless office to receive a cable: "Mother and daughter (Catherine) doing well". So, a rapid celebration party.

The day before we were due to arrive in Singapore we learnt that Indonesian insurgents had taken over some Malayan villages in Borneo, so in effect we were at war with President Suharto's Indonesia. On arrival at Singapore we embarked a regiment of Ghurkhas and proceeded at 27 knots to land them on a decidedly dodgy jetty at Labuan.

The dodgy jetty at Labuan

Then we learnt the full horror of the situation. Hundreds of insurgents had crossed into British North Borneo from Indonesian South Borneo and were laying waste to many of the villages deep into the jungle. A platoon of Ghurkhas had been ambushed in one of the villages, ten of them being killed. This happened the day before we arrived. The Ghurkhas we landed proceeded immediately to this village, and rounded up the villagers. The village headman was asked who was responsible for the ambush, he denied all knowledge, so it was out with a Ghurkha kukri and off with his head!

TIGER landing Ghurkhas at Labuan, British North Borneo

TIGER landing Ghurkhas at Labuan, British North Borneo

The deputy headman was then asked the same question and very quickly provided the required information. I don't know what happened to the ambushers, but I don't suppose it was anything very pleasant.

Christmas was spent alongside in Singapore. Without families these occasions are always rather forced. However the Officers were allocated a fellow officer and had to buy a present for him for less than £1, usually it was something jokey and where better to find it than Singapore.

We had a lot of keen golfers in TIGER. If we couldn't get onto a golf course we had a ruse for practising our driving. We stuck the tees in the corking on the Quarterdeck. One evening when I was Officer of the Watch we established a competition to see who could land a ball on the HARTLAND POINT, a repair ship at a buoy 200 yards out in the harbour. Someone obviously succeeded because I got a very irate phone call from the Officer of the Day on HARTLAND POINT complaining that someone from the flagship was driving golf balls at them. I said I would investigate, suggesting that this was most unlikely. End of competition!

On 27th December we left Singapore for a farewell visit to Hong Kong for a few days. Then down to Subic Bay in the Philippines, the base of the US Seventh fleet. The bars in Alongapo were the crudest of any that I had visited anywhere. The antics of the bar girls were pretty unspeakable. Why did I go there? All part of one's education?!

On the passage home TIGER wouldn't have been the ship that she was if she hadn't managed to fit in a few visits. After leaving Singapore we stopped at the Andaman Islands off the coast of Burma but, I believe, owned by India. The islands are very low-lying and inhabited by a number of very primitive tribes (some of which are believed to have been wiped out in the 2005 tsunami). I have no idea what the purpose of TIGER's visit was. Cruise ships visit there these days, I presume for the scenery?

Next stop was Madras. Nothing much had changed since my visit 8 years previously, except that it was even more difficult for the sailors to get a beer ashore. Some of the officers were invited by the local Indian General to a reception in their Officer's mess, a superb building dating from the days of the Raj. After a long wait soft drinks arrived. By 8pm there was no sign of any food or any other officers except the General and his Aide de Camp. It turned out that the younger officers had stated that they didn't wish to entertain the British, but the General had not had the courage to cancel the occasion. We just managed to get to the Gymkhana Club in time to have a very poor Madras curry. We felt sorry for the General who obviously wanted to do his best by the British. He had been in Hobson's Horse, a famous Indian Army regiment, and to have a lot of bolshie officers to command can't have been much fun.

Our passage across the Indian Ocean towards Aden was a surreal experience. The Cuban Missile Crisis was in full swing and we were kept informed of events on an hourly basis. I remember thinking that if there was a nuclear holocaust we were probably in the best place to survive. However what good would that do us if the rest of the human race had been exterminated?

Aden, Suez Canal, Malta, Gibraltar and home to Plymouth on 23rd March 1963. What a wonderful welcome with 3-month old new daughter and new house in Hampshire to inspect! Naval wives have to be even more resourceful than other service wives. The year away in the TIGER had been full of interest and travelling. I was particularly fortunate to have had two fly ahead Fleet visit planning excursions. This ensured that I did not become too bored with the endless watch-keeping. The officers were probably the most able I ever served with, and several went on to achieve high rank. Although it was a very efficient ship it was also a very relaxed and sociable one. I have nothing but fond memories of my time in the TIGER.

Chapter 14
HMS MERCURY, East Meon, Hampshire
May 1963 to April 1964
Lieutenant

All Executive (Seaman) Officers were required to sub-specialise. Communications Officers considered themselves to be a cut above the rest of Naval Officers, rather like the cavalry in the Army. However they came in two sorts, the rather grand with aristocratic pretensions who were renowned for sporting white silk handkerchiefs with their uniform, and those with an abiding interest in the technology. I fitted into neither category using the year's course to establish a home (at Meonstoke in Hampshire) for the first time and to provide myself with sufficient technical knowledge to fulfil a communications career. At the time I had no idea how useful this would also prove in civilian life.

The course was centred in a stately home near Petersfield which the Navy had commandeered during the Second World War from a family of linoleum manufacturers. The Navy had surrounded the imposing house and gardens with Nissen huts and very ugly 1950's buildings to provide sufficient space for training communications officers and ratings.

The course itself was relatively undemanding. The syllabus consisted of radio communications, short and long distance, but it was valve technology, being immediately before the arrival of satellite and digital techniques. A significant proportion of the course was devoted to flag signalling for controlling ship manoeuvres, semaphore and Morse, which was what some senior officers understood from their World War II experience. The ability to control ships manoeuvring close together was important but the cynic in me comments that there was a fair element of 'being good at fighting a previous war'.

However the course did include a very good section on electronic warfare, essentially the interception and jamming of enemy transmissions. At that time Royal Navy shipboard equipment probably led the world in this field.

The great joy of the Long Signal Course was the social life and living only four miles away from the school. The Officers had shooting rights over three tracts of land: at South Harting, where we reared 200 pheasants in two stretches of woodland; at the Signal School itself, which provided two afternoons of rough shooting; and at Winterslow near Salisbury, which was only rough shooting but contained everything from deer to pheasants to pigeon.

Summer and winter balls were the highlight of the social season. The Long Signal Course officers were expected to organise the decorations, each year being more elaborate than the last.

At the end of the course we were asked where we would like to serve next, rather depending upon one's position in the end of course exams. I only managed the middle order, which wasn't bad considering how little effort I had put in. As a result I was sent to do a two-year exchange with the Australian Navy, which suited Rosemary and me just fine.

We must have been the most unsuccessful Long Signal Course intake. Out of fourteen, only one reached Captain's rank, 3 died within 5 years of completing the course and only one completed a full naval career.

Chapter 15
Two-Year Exchange, Australia
May 1964 to April 1966
Lieutenant-Commander

During the Long Communications Course I had mentioned to my Course Officer that, as I had family in Australia, I wouldn't mind doing an exchange in the Royal Australian Navy (RAN) for a couple of years. This was not a career-enhancing move as the more ambitious went off to be Flag Lieutenants to Admirals in the Home Fleet, and that sort of thing.

With two small children we flew to Australia. Friends in Singapore looked after us during a three-day stopover which was the saving grace for a very long air trip. We were the first to go out to Australia by Air Trooping with the Royal Air Force. Previously everybody had enjoyed six weeks on a P & O liner, so we weren't very happy about that.

On arrival in Sydney I was told that I had to fly to Melbourne the next day to join HMAS DERWENT, which was just finishing being built there. Rosemary was left to find us accommodation in Sydney, which she did very successfully, choosing a nice house in Rose Bay not far from the golf course and Doyle's fish restaurant. In fact there was no need for me to fly to Melbourne in such a rush as we didn't go to sea until weeks later. However that was very typical of the way the Royal Australian Navy managed its people. The year before I arrived, the carrier MELBOURNE had run over the destroyer VOYAGER with the loss of 200 lives. The Australian Navy was never held in very high regard by the Australians. Nobody was ever court-martialled or blamed for this event, further reducing the RAN's public standing.

Joining a new ship as Operations and Communications officer should have been exciting, but the latest radar jamming equipment which we were supposed to trial was not fitted. So the course I did in the UK before setting out proved rather pointless. After sea trials and a short workup, we did a tour of the state capitals - Perth, Hobart, Sydney and Brisbane - to show off the RAN's latest ship. It seemed my naval career was punctuated by visits to these cities, but this was the only occasion that I visited Brisbane while afloat.

HMAS DERWENT firing Seacat missile

The Australians always had at least two ships operating with the Royal Navy's Far East Fleet based in Singapore. So DERWENT was sent 'up north' for a six-month stint. In those days, before the emergence of their Islamic ambitions, the Indonesians, under President Sukarno, were trying to achieve dominance in the Singapore area. They represented a considerable naval threat, possessing several Russian-built, missile-firing patrol boats which could potentially do very considerable damage to larger British/Australian warships. Fortunately, although we didn't know it at the time, the Russians hadn't shown the Indonesians how to use these boats, and probably kept them deliberately starved of spares. Had the Indonesians had firing ability, the jamming device the DERWENT should have been fitted with would have come in very handy.

On the way up to Singapore the DERWENT stopped at the island of Manus, one of the largest natural harbours in the world and the scene of much conflict with the Japanese during World War II. It was essentially a refuelling station but had a small Australian Navy staff. The people who were sent there enjoyed(?) an isolated tropical island existence, being at least 1000 miles from anywhere and away from Australia for up to three years. It was not unknown for chaps to become a little peculiar. The channel in and out of Manus had to be followed very carefully as there were literally hundreds of wrecked ships in the harbour.

For the first time in my naval career, I fell out with my Captain. He was small in stature and had a monumental "chip on his shoulder", as did quite a few Australians at that time. He was determined to make a name for himself as a hard man. While preparing for an exercise alongside in Singapore, he decided to confine me to my cabin, for an alleged misdemeanour the details of which I can't recall. Eventually he relented when I pointed out that as Operations Officer, it was difficult to prepare for an exercise from my cabin. He was loathed by the officers but the Aussie sailors rather liked the tough man image. The state of my relations with the Captain was typified by a remark made to me by the Leading Seaman in charge of the Operations Room. "Sir, you shouldn't look down your nose at the Captain like that." I didn't even realise that I was! This was the same Leading Seaman who made life more bearable in times of stress with the immortal words: "Would you loik a brew, sir?". We did a lot of very tedious patrolling against Indonesian terrorists around Borneo and in the Singapore Straits. However, we did have one lively little incident. I was on the bridge one night when a terrorist in a sampan opened fire on the bridge with an Armalite rifle. His bullets passed straight through the aluminium superstructure and were pinging around the bridge. The sailor manning the Bren gun on the roof of the bridge disposed of the sampan and its contents very quickly. So I feel I earned the only medal I have, the Malayan General Service Medal. I was very happy indeed to leave the DERWENT on returning to Sydney and to have a very pleasant shore job.

The Australian Joint Anti-Submarine School (AJASS) was located 120 miles south of Sydney on the edge of the RAN's only Fleet Air Arm station at Nowra. Its purpose was to instruct ships' operations teams before they went to workup for operational service. The staff were half Australian Navy and half Australian Air Force, with an American nuclear submariner to lecture on submarine warfare. My job was to give a one-hour talk, in conjunction with my RAAF colleague, on Communications and Electronic Warfare . This took place once a week on average, not exactly demanding.

AJASS Staff

Most of the Australian Navy ships were not that well equipped with electronic warfare systems and the communications fits were pretty standard throughout their Fleet. So, to keep the audience interested in the heat after lunch was a challenge. My RAAF colleague and I developed a dialogue that seemed to be both informative and entertaining.

The housing situation was challenging. My predecessor rented a beach house on Jervis Bay at a village called Huskisson, and we chose to take it on from him. It was 15 miles through the bush to the nearest town

Nowra. Our eldest child Tim's first school was the Huskisson Primary School where he acquired some 'interesting' Australian expressions. Life in Australia outside the cities could be quite basic. We only had a privy down the garden. It was as well to examine what was under the seat before sitting down. A visitor reported having seen a lethal spider on one occasion.

In 1965, the white Australia policy was still very much in force. Non-white immigrants were not allowed in. A lot of aboriginal children were 'adopted' by white Australian families. Many of those who weren't, were left out in the bush where nobody cared very much about them. 'Abos' were largely a source of silly stories.

We had a jetty at the end of the garden which was on a creek flowing into Jervis Bay. Essentially Huskisson was a fishing village, with a few shops, pub, Returned Serviceman's League Club and school. One day the fishermen shot a shark, about 5 feet long, which they placed on our jetty. We sat the two children (5 and 3) by it and took a photo that was sent back to Salisbury. This produced a panic telegram, grandparents wondering what on earth we were doing to their grandchildren.

Many years after we left, large parts of Huskisson were destroyed by a bush fire, but, being close to the sea, we were never at risk. One of the serious hazards was kangaroos crossing the road at night. The kangaroos were big and could easily write off a car and its occupants. There always seemed to be more of them when driving home after mess dinners! One such dinner led to a chair "accidentally" striking me across the nose which was rather unfortunate as the following day we were going to Sydney for their spectacular Easter Show. I spent five days in the Naval Hospital at Balmoral while the family enjoyed the best Australian agriculture could offer.

There were two other Brits on the Air Station, a helicopter pilot who went on to become First Sea Lord, and an RAF Squadron Leader. Socially we saw very little of them. At weekends we tended to go to a beautiful sandy cove for barbecues and huge quantities of beer. One's contribution to a picnic consisted of a case of Resch's chilled beer bought from the pub, i.e. 12 large bottles, the average Aussie bloke's consumption during a Sunday.

A very happy memory of Huskisson was chipping oysters off the rocks at the bottom of the garden. We had so many that we used to cook them Kilpatrick, with chopped pieces of bacon and Lea & Perrins. One night we went prawning in St George's Basin, not far from Huskisson. You had to wait till the full moon when the prawns 'ran' best. With nets we filled buckets with medium-sized prawns then cooked and ate them straight away. Delicious.

Distances in Australia are enormous, so one had to wait for periods of leave before tackling major expeditions. We did manage to visit the Blue Mountains several times, Adelaide, Melbourne, Canberra, Wagga Wagga and Hay. One of the properties we visited was very palatial, but most were just simple houses (bungalows) set in the wonderful Australian landscape. I haven't included pictures of Australian life because that is a whole memoir of its own.

The thought of Air Trooping home with the Royal Air Force and two now not so small children filled us with gloom. I wrote to the Admiralty asking permission to travel home from Sydney to the UK across the USA, provided that I paid the difference in cost. To our amazement they agreed. So we embarked in the "ORIANA" at Sydney and were able to take our car and luggage with us for nothing. Three weeks first class P & O was a marvellous experience, luxury we had never previously achieved. We disembarked at San Francisco and visited friends at Palo Alto and Baltimore before flying home. The cost for the four of us was £250.

Chapter 16
Faslane, Scotland
April 1966 to June 1968
Lieutenant-Commander

In April 1966 I took up my post as Polaris Communications Officer in Faslane, situated on the Gareloch some 25 miles north of Glasgow. In many ways this was undeniably the most responsible job I was ever asked to undertake in the Royal Navy.

My main duties were:
- To ensure that the Polaris submarine communications functioned correctly, in particular so that HMS RESOLUTION could deploy on patrol on time on 1 June 1967 with all her communications working correctly.
- To oversee the working up of other submarines, both nuclear and conventional, to operational efficiency from a communications and electronic warfare point of view, before they deployed to their squadrons.
- To supervise the working of the communications centre at Faslane and outlying radio stations.

Not being a submarine trained officer, for experience I was offered the chance to 'ride' HMS VALIANT, a nuclear attack submarine, from Chatham to Faslane. This was only a three-day trip going outside Ireland, so you can imagine the speed we went, staying virtually submerged throughout. I slept in the torpedo compartment forward, strangely quiet even at a speed of 20 knots plus.

I concentrated on understanding how the broadcast schedules every four hours were read and the procedure for making radio transmissions, so that the Operations Room at Faslane could know that the submarine was safe and sound.

HMS MAIDSTONE

For the first three months I lived in the World War II submarine depot ship HMS MAIDSTONE, as the Wardroom and married quarters were not yet complete. During this period we commissioned the new Communications Centre ashore, which was linked to the Fleet Headquarters at Northwood, Middlesex, from where the Polaris deterrent was controlled.

Much of the Royal Navy, including many senior officers, was decidedly unenthusiastic about being responsible for the deterrent, principally for budgetary reasons. For my first few months I had a series of Polaris programme deadlines to meet. Failure to meet a deadline required me to report personally to Vice-Admiral Polaris in the Ministry of Defence how I intended to resolve the problem. Happily I never had to do that.

As a lowly Lieutenant-Commander I often had to invite some very senior "gentlemen" in the communications world to provide me with equipment at a few hours' notice. For an MOD procurement process, which had never delivered anything on time, this was very definitely counter-culture! You can understand that I was not very popular with my seniors, as Polaris was taking away great slices of their budget.

Just to explain, the deterrent depends entirely on secure communications containing the order to fire, if it comes to that. The order-to-fire signal has to be received in a full and complete format. Once the missiles have been fired – God forbid – the fact that they have been fired has to be transmitted to the Prime Minister and acknowledged. The communications network ashore required several backups. At the time I was assisting in installing all this. The British Telecom (GPO) engineers were strongly opposed to the whole Polaris process and so we had to replace some of them with serving RN ratings. Nobody ever explained what my powers actually were, so, if I felt something needed doing, I didn't hesitate to do it. I didn't have time for lengthy bureaucratic discussions with civil servants and the unions. You can imagine that there were a number of noses put out of joint. In any event, RESOLUTION went to sea on time and the first generation of naval deterrent was under way.

Just before this we had a visit from Denis Healey, the Defence Secretary, who was given a full briefing about the deterrent. During the briefing I was on duty in the Operations Room when the Red (secure) phone to Number 10 Downing Street rang.

"Prime Minister (i.e. Harold Wilson) here. Could I speak to the Defence Secretary?"

"I will go and fetch him, Prime Minister."

"Defence Secretary. The Prime Minister is on the red phone."

"Thank you. I wonder what the bugger (sic) wants now."

Shock horror from the author accustomed to giving politicians due respect!

One of the joys of working at Faslane was that I had three senior submarine Captains to report to. Two of these were the most distinguished officers of their generation. One became Chief of the Defence Staff and the other Second Sea Lord. Not being a submariner, I often had to ask their opinion about some problem I had. They usually came up with good ideas. I can honestly say I have never worked for more brilliant bosses, inside or outside the Navy. I mention this because the impression created to the general public by many senior officers carrying out their duties is not always what it might be, mainly I believe because of their lack of experience of the world outside the Royal Navy.

One day the Commodore in charge of the Faslane Naval Base sent for me and said that the Director of Naval Security, a Royal Marine colonel, in London wished to see me urgently. With fear and trepidation I took the next civilian flight south – a huge expense in those days – to see him at 1000 next morning. I was ushered into his office feeling extremely nervous. Nobody had given me the least idea what the problem was.

"Sit down, Allen. While you were serving in Singapore you took a girl who was not your wife to Bangkok for the weekend. Furthermore you were engaged in several wife swap parties in Singapore, and various other activities of a sexual nature".

"Colonel, I am sorry to disappoint you but the chap you are talking about has obviously led a more exciting life than me but I am not he."

"Steve (his deputy and my divisional officer in the DEVONSHIRE), show Lt Cdr Allen out."

"Thank you, Colonel, for giving me the opportunity to visit my tailor. Would you like to come out to lunch?"

"You won't mention this to anyone, will you?"

"Of course not. I'll dine out on it for months!"

The next major event was a trip to sea in the REPULSE, the second of the Polaris boats, during the course of her operational trials. We surfaced head to sea in the Atlantic off the Mull of Kintyre. On opening the conning tower hatch, we were struck by one of those one-in-a-million waves you hear about from round the world yachtsmen. A huge amount of water was taken aboard – we were paddling in the wireless office – and I wondered whether we had enough buoyancy to get back to harbour. Obviously we did, but the mixture of salt water and electronics took a while to sort out. As a non-submariner I was somewhat disconcerted.

Life at Faslane was not all work. I was the Shooting Secretary for the

Base. This amounted to having the shooting rights over a vast track of un-keepered grouse moor owned by the MOD. It was lovely country with fabulous views over the Gareloch and the Holy Loch, but a very long walk produced perhaps half a dozen birds.

Rather more productive was the Army's TA range on the eastern side of the Gareloch with a degree of keeping and well established butts. We used to have bags of 20 brace or more.

In January several times we drove up to Appin, near Oban, taking the ferry to Lismore island. The party consisted of a retired submarine Admiral, a retired Lieutenant-Colonel and myself, the driver. Great skeins of geese (pink foot and Brent) lived on Lismore in the winter. In six visits we only managed to shoot one goose which fell about 200 yards out to sea. None of the dogs could be persuaded to go out and fetch it, so the Admiral stripped off and retrieved the bird he had shot. I think the sea was frozen in parts!

The married quarters in Rhu

Living in married quarters was a new experience for us. In the usual Ministry of Defence manner, the cheapest quote got the job to build these quarters. In January 1967 the site was struck by the tail end of a

Caribbean hurricane with winds of more than 120mph. Many of the aluminium roofs were peeled off as if by a can opener, fortunately not ours. This storm took place in the middle of the night. We set up our house as a temporary dormitory. In the morning we realised the full extent of the damage. About half the houses had lost their roofs and a huge tree blocked the entrance to the estate. The electricity remained off for 24 hours, so the Base established an emergency soup kitchen. Now we know why the Scots build themselves substantial stone houses.

Our time at Faslane was at the height of the Cold War. The Russians operated about 150 submarines from Murmansk. Some were nuclear missile boats deployed off the east coast of the United States. Some were hunter killer submarines which often tried to track our Polaris boats. The remainder were conventional submarines which were in the habit of trying to disrupt NATO exercises. So, to be prepared for the possibility of a war against the Russians, we used to carry out surveillance of their seagoing activities. In the Operations Room we were aware when a submarine was away on this sort of operation, but no details.

In the middle of one night while on duty in the Operations Room, I received a telephone call from the First Lieutenant of a nuclear submarine who had been away on one of these missions.

"Tim, where are you?"

"Alongside in Loch Ewe (a fuelling depot in NW Scotland). Basically, we had an underwater collision with a Russian submarine which removed our conning tower. Could you inform everyone who needs to know? Luckily there are no casualties."

So that the submarine could return to Faslane for repair, a makeshift conning tower was constructed at Loch Ewe, so that the public would not know that anything was amiss.

History doesn't relate what happened to the Russian submarine. The Russians didn't report accidents unless they were already in the public domain. The chap on the other end of the phone at Loch Ewe joined the Navy with me in 1949. So I had a full description of events later on. It was very interesting to hear how people reacted in very stressful circumstances.

Rosemary and I thoroughly enjoyed our two years in Scotland. One highlight was meeting the Queen Mother when she commissioned HMS NEPTUNE. However, in many ways it was more foreign than living in Australia. I'm afraid we didn't really integrate well with the locals, partly because of the very long hours I worked and because our small children – our second son, Nicholas, was born in Helensburgh on 8 December 1967 – were very time-consuming. This was one of the few jobs in the Royal Navy where you were given a job and you could see it through to a successful conclusion. Getting the deterrent to sea in full working order on time gave a great deal of satisfaction.

Chapter 17
HMS ALBION
August 1968 to August 1969
Lieutenant-Commander

Continuing my principle of always going where my appointer wished, at the end of two very demanding years doing Polaris communications, I was sent to join the Commando Carrier ALBION in the Far East. Joining a ship in mid-commission is never easy, especially becoming part of an established team of officers who had made their own mark with the ship's senior officers. The prospect of spending another year away from the family was not too cheering either.

I began to realise that, having spent two years rubbing up a lot of senior officers the wrong way followed by this rump end commission appointment, my promotion prospects were beginning to dwindle. I decided to take a correspondence course on basic accountancy out with me. This proved very useful after I left the Navy.

I flew out to join the ship in Singapore by Royal Air Force transport ("Crab Air") from Brize Norton via Gan, an island in the middle of the Indian Ocean. I always reckoned that the RAF only had this place to try and convince Defence Ministers that they had a worldwide reach. Anyway it was shut down not long after I passed through.

A Commando Carrier's main aim in life was to embark a Royal Marine Commando, 650 officers and men with their vehicles, communications and light artillery, and put them ashore wherever they were needed. The Communications Plan was my responsibility. It had to cater for ship/shore/ship communications, mainly voice, and the commando's internal communications, so it was a fairly complex document.

HMS ALBION as a Commando Carrier

Helicopter operating on HMS ALBION

When the Commando embarked it become very crowded on board, virtually doubling the number of people in the ship. In spite of this, relations between the Royal Marines (nicknamed "bootnecks") and the sailors were pretty good. The Royal Marines are part of the Royal Navy but they do tend to behave more like soldiers. I remember the Commander coming down to breakfast in his Wardroom (Officer's Mess) one morning to find that a young Royal Marine officer had his boots on the table. The gentleman was advised of the error of his ways and was not able to finish his breakfast!

ALBION was an extremely happy ship. Most of the officers were not expecting to be promoted and so there was not the jockeying for position which sometimes occurs. Many of the senior ratings were very experienced which made my life easy. In harbour and at sea, there were so many seaman officers that watch-keeping duties didn't come round very often. A typical day in Singapore might consist of a morning's work on board (0700 to 1300), lunch at the Officer's Club – a very good line in steak sandwiches and Tiger beer - a game of mixed doubles tennis

HMS ALBION entering Singapore

with a school teacher as partner, down to Singapore town by taxi for a spot of shopping, and a Chinese supper afterwards. A tough life indeed. At this time, after a long period of colonial rule, Singapore was starting to become one of the great commercial powerhouses of the world. Under the British it had had multiple racial problems, being a mix of Chinese, Malay and Indian, with a few other nation expats as well. The British had never managed to make the mix gel very well. By 1969, Premier Lee Kwan Yue was ruling the island with an authoritarian regime, although technically the nation was still a democracy. From outside the liberals mocked what he was doing, but he managed to create an extraordinarily prosperous country with a standard of living way above that of many countries in Europe. Singapore was very far removed from the rather scruffy island many of us remembered from previous visits. Because it was becoming so successful, the worry was that countries like Indonesia and Malaysia might try and subsume it in some way. As a result, Singapore had armed forces way beyond its obvious requirements. The dual carriageway leading up to the new airport could be converted to

HMS ALBION alongside in Hong Kong

a runway in four hours . Happily that was never very likely to happen. The ship undertook a very varied programme of port visits – Hong Kong (twice), Kobe and Nagoya in Japan, Perth, WA, and of course many periods at the Singapore Naval Base. The visit to Kobe was a high spot. We persuaded the Commander that it would be a good scheme if he put the ship's Land Rover at our disposal for a few days. So, four officers set off for the interior of Japan. One of our number was a Japanese interpreter, a very rare animal in the Royal Navy. We arrived at a small village about 100 miles from Kobe and found a ryokan, a small country inn, complete with natural hot springs. The management confirmed that four naval officers could be accommodated, and we were duly shown to the height of discomfort, straw mattresses on the floor, in a sparsely furnished room. The Gunnery Officer decided that he needed a haircut, so we all trouped down to the village barber to view this spectacle, and so did the entire population of the village, or so it seemed. In 1969 many of them had never seen a European before, and certainly not one having his hair cut.

Japanese temples at Kyoto; see also full page colour photograph on page 190

The next move was to sample the natural springs. We took our bathing costumes but these were not required. So we joined with the villagers of all ages splashing about in the very warm baths. Very pointed gestures suggested that they were amazed that our bodies were constructed in a similar manner to theirs.

The only way to get to sleep on the floor was to empty the two bottles of whisky we had brought with us. That may not have been a good idea. A confrontation with raw fish for breakfast was a considerable challenge.
See Photograph on Page 191.

My umpteenth visit to Perth, Western Australia, enabled me to catch up with lots of friends from the past. Then we set off for the long slog home across the Indian Ocean, stopping at Durban to refuel. We had a splendid day at Durban races with the Oppenheimer family.

We had a very exciting return to Portsmouth, after eleven months away. As was typical with my ships, ALBION went to the scrap yard shortly after our return .

Chapter 18
HMS ACHILLES
September 1969 to March 1971
Lieutenant-Commander

Attending an ALBION officer's wedding in Hampshire, September 1969

In September 1969, I was appointed First Lieutenant and Second in Command of HMS ACHILLES. I travelled up to Messrs Yarrow's shipyard in Scotstoun, Glasgow to find that the ship was about six months away from completion. ACHILLES was the second last of the Leander class of frigate. We had some opportunity to determine the finish inside, e.g. regarding the layout of the Wardroom, a very important matter.

I chose to live in the Royal Northern Yacht Club at Rhu on the Gareloch. I had some knowledge of this area from my time doing the Polaris job. The Club chef would come to see me at breakfast so that I could choose my supper menu. In the evenings I consumed copious quantities of Glenlivet with the locals. Driving the twenty miles into Glasgow in the early morning was particularly challenging in the snow and dark of a horrendous Scottish winter. However, I seemed to manage it without "metal hitting metal". Rosemary chose to live at home in Hampshire with our three children rather than removing to a married quarter in Paisley, a very sensible decision.

Normally, the First Lieutenant had been in charge of the day-to-day running of the ship's activities, some 250 personnel. However ACHILLES had been selected as the trial ship for a new management system that involved the four departmental heads drawing up a weekly and monthly programme for running the ship. Departmental heads had very precise job descriptions and objectives set for each month and these were compared with actual achievement. Unlike business management, upon which these principles were based, the ship's programme involved numerous changes and enabled unachieved objectives to be easily explained away! However the integration of departmental activities brought enormous benefits to all once the senior ratings had been persuaded to embrace the new planning process. From my own point of view, I used these principles when running a much bigger show in Paris for British Telecom. Looking back, this was something of a revolution, virtually the first practical change in running a ship since Nelson's day.

My personal memories of my time on Clydeside include the calls of "Hey, Wully" and the many incomprehensible Glaswegian accents. The pop singer Lulu, the singer, then aged 15, was already entertaining the sailors in the local pubs. Then there was playing three-card brag from Euston to Glasgow on the night sleeper and travelling south at high speed just in time to miss the arrival of our fourth child, third son, William.

Launch of HMS ACHILLES at Yarrow (Shipbuilders) Ltd, 21st November 1968

Work-wise, I had to plan for the Commissioning of the ship. Not the least of my problems was to get the Battle Honours Board agreed by the Admiralty. A ship with a famous name like ACHILLES had almost as many battle honours as the ARK ROYAL. Her immediate predecessor had taken part in the Battle of the River Plate and had been manned by the New Zealand Navy through much of the 1940's and 1950's.

Eventually this enormous board was constructed, brass on wood, and had to be polished every day.

By a constant process of badgering we managed to get the ship more or less completed and ready for sea trials. The shipbuilders weren't keen to let us go as they only had one more half-built ship on their order books. The Clydeside yards were running down fast so they wanted to keep the work going.

HMS ACHILLES on sea trials in the Clyde, 1970

Sea Acceptance Trials were duly completed without too many alarms. The Captain joined the ship and we sailed down to home base Devonport, hugely inconvenient for most of us who lived in the Portsmouth area. The ship was commissioned by the First Sea Lord, whose son joined us not long after. No fewer than eleven full admirals, who had served in the previous ACHILLES, attended the ceremony.

Workup which followed was a four-week period whereby the ship's efficiency as a fighting unit was tested. This was probably the most rigorous proving of warships and their crew anywhere in the world and involved countering simultaneous air, surface and submarine threats.

The Commissioning Ceremony of HMS Achilles, Commander Kelly Lowe and myself (right)

We emerged with a 'good', a rating awarded to very few ships. However, looking back, the ship's only defence against any form of missile attack was chaff (radar confusion) or gunfire. The ship fought in defence watches, 6 hours on, 6 hours off, so could sustain action for quite long periods. The most useful weapon was the Wasp helicopter, which could be despatched well away from the ship to deal with surface or submarine targets with air-launched torpedoes.

Before we were deployed to the Far East we had to practise our entertaining arrangements, e.g. turning the Wardroom into a night club. So we made port visits to Le Havre, Port Talbot and Glasgow. This Naval Officer had organised more cocktail parties than most Naval Officers had ever thought about, so it wasn't a great test for me.

We left Devonport in March for the Far East accompanied by the frigate DANAE, whose First Lieutenant had been a Midshipman with me in the CEYLON. We sailed south via Gibraltar and Simonstown in South Africa to take up our duties as Beira patrol ship, off the coast of

Mayor of Port Talbot on the helicopter deck

Mozambique. This was really the first opportunity to bed in the new management system, and to discover whether it was flexible enough to run a warship. King Neptune had to initiate those who had not crossed the Equator before, about half the ship's company.

Rhodesia (now Zimbabwe) was ruled at that time by a white farmer called Smith. Both parties in the UK government were busy promoting the "africanisation" of Africa, and were keen to subvert Mr Smith's regime wherever possible. It was thought that the oil for Rhodesia went through the port of Beira in Mozambique therefore we were invited to stop all tankers heading there. I suppose our blockade must have worked because we never saw a tanker in 11 extremely boring weeks. In fact it transpired that Mr Smith got his oil from South Africa, so our efforts were even more meaningless. It is interesting to reflect that Mr Smith's regime was opposed by one Robert Mugabe who has become one of the most bestial tyrants that Africa has known. And at the time we were doing our best to help him!

Twin refuelling at sea with HMS ACHILLES, HMS BULWARK and GOLD RANGER

Concerning the conflict with Mr Smith, a little story. At the beginning of this confrontation the carrier EAGLE was dispatched to see if the arrival of a carrier on the scene would frighten Mr Smith into submission. The EAGLE was fitted with the first secure satellite voice system connected directly to the Ministry of Defence in Whitehall. The Minister of Defence at that time, Denis Healey, decided that he would like to exercise his authority directly and so asked to be connected to the EAGLE.

Minister – "Captain, I would like you to bomb the railway lines in Rhodesia."

Captain (a well known Scottish laird) – "Minister, I only take my orders from the First Sea Lord. In any case, many of my family live in Rhodesia and I am not about to bomb them".

This, I understand, was a useful precedent that reinforced why Ministers should lay down political policy but that military orders should always be issued by serving officers.

Taking the con in command of HMS ACHILLES – briefly

The eleven weeks of Beira patrol proved a particularly testing time for me. Tradition has it that the Captain delegates the running of the ship to his officers while attending to operational and navigational matters himself. My Captain was an officer who had made his way in the world from humble beginnings. He was not capable of occupying himself in his cabin, and I suffered constant interference. In particular, the Officers complained that he was always in the Wardroom not allowing them the freedom of conversation that they might wish. Tradition has it that the Captain only enters the Wardroom when invited. So in the end I had to ask him to conform to normal naval practice, a stricture he didn't accept very willingly.

Worse was to follow. The Captain was convinced that homosexuality was rife on board. At that time homosexuality was a Court Martial offence in the Navy. The First Lieutenant was required to be the prosecuting officer in all serious charges. I had brought before me a charge against a Leading Seaman who was alleged to have committed offences against a Junior Seaman. The only evidence was of good natured 'fondling'. I decided that, although there was hardly a case to answer, the matter should be brought before the Captain. He had to dismiss the case as I had warned him he would. He was furious because I had made him look foolish. It certainly put an end to matters homosexual and ideas thereof! I mention these internal conflicts which can occur when two strong-minded individuals are thrust together in a small ship, particularly during a pointless and unrewarding activity such as the Beira patrol.

The patrol was duly completed and we were allowed a week of rest and recreation at Mombasa in Kenya. It had the most sensational white sandy beaches and a good supply of bars and entertainment to enable the Ship's Company to recover from the tedium of the previous weeks.

HMS ACHILLES entering Singapore Naval Base

From there we steamed steadily to Singapore where I turned over to my relief. I had had eighteen months with ACHILLES, of which twelve months were at sea. In spite of my later travails with the Captain, I had enjoyed the time enormously; it is always a bit special commissioning a new ship.

Chapter 19
HMS TAMAR, Hong Kong
April 1971 to April 1973
Lieutenant-Commander

Having left the ACHILLES in Singapore, I flew home for Christmas 1970 and a few weeks' leave. The prospect of going to Hong Kong for two years as Staff Communications Officer was immensely appealing, not least because it meant having lots of time with the children. The only drawback was having the two elder ones travelling back and forth to boarding school in the UK, something with which they coped quite admirably.

By the time we arrived in 1971, the Royal Navy had virtually withdrawn from Singapore, so the Fleet's communications were being run from Hong Kong. There were relatively few RN ships to provide for, the occasional visiting squadron and the Hong Kong guardship. In 1971, Hong Kong was functioning like most other colonies. The Governor was the Queen's representative and the Colonial Secretary was the head of the appointed Legislative Council. However, even then, everyone was conscious that the Chinese would take the Colony back in 1997 when the lease expired.

The most extraordinary thing was the way the Chinese commercial expertise and the British ability to maintain law and order melded together in a harmonious fashion. The Communist riots of the '60s, largely generated because more illegal immigrants were coming into the Colony than could be accommodated, were a thing of the past.

The Colony consisted of Hong Kong island, smaller than the Isle of Wight, and the New Territories, approx 600 square miles bordering mainland China. Into this small space were crammed 5 million Chinese and 100,000 expats and other nationalities. The Army were charged with preventing incursions into Hong Kong from mainland China, a task which everyone freely admitted could only be achieved with the co-operation of the Chinese.

The Chinese were keen that Hong Kong should continue as it was, because, before the resurrection of Shanghai, Hong Kong was the commercial and financial path to and from China itself. The Hong Kong and Shanghai Banking Corporation (HSBC) became immensely wealthy, powerful and influential from this time on. A good proportion of the wealth of today's City of London emanates from these times.

In the way that the Ministry of Defence operates, with absurdly long procurement timetables, I arrived to find that they were busy building new communications centres and transmitting stations, when what they really needed were mobile satellite terminals. However I was able to invite the head of Service Signals, an admiral, out from the UK to open these facilities. While he was in Hong Kong I had a memorable conversation with him:

Admiral: "Do you know, David, I've had an absolutely miserable career in the Royal Navy because I've always been seeking promotion."

Self: "I've had a wonderfully happy naval career, always going where my appointer sent me, and not really worrying whether anybody would remember to promote me." (Which, as it happens, they didn't.) I don't know what the moral of this tale is, you can decide!

One of my sideline jobs was as Naval Aide de Camp (ADC) to the Governor, a very posh uniform *(Photo page 192)*. The Governor, Sir Murray MacLehose (known as "Jock the Sock"), had been in the Royal Naval Volunteer Reserve (RNVR) during the war and was therefore very pro-Navy and ever so slightly anti-Army. My duties consisted of assisting at various dinner parties, accompanying the Governor on specific occasions and, most memorably, as part of a small team who organised the week-long visit of Princess Anne to Hong Kong. As a reward, R and I were able to have lunch with HRH. This was the first solo overseas visit by the Princess Royal and so we were even more keen to make sure that everything went according to plan. We needn't have worried, she charmed everybody with her quick quips and good humour.

As ADC, I needed to sign the Commander British Forces' book. I hoped to do this surreptitiously as this particular General had been sent home from a grouse shoot by my father (in my presence) for dangerous shooting.

General: "We've never met, have we?"

Self: "No, General, never." (We both knew we were being economical with the truth!)

Domestic life in Hong Kong at that time was probably as good as it gets. Our married quarters were a spacious flat on Stubbs Road, half way up The Peak, opposite Han Suyin house, made famous in the film "Love is a Many Splendoured Thing" and the most photographed house on the Island *(Photo page 192)*. With an "amah" (Chinese maid) to look after the children – the youngest spoke Cantonese before he spoke English – we were free to amuse ourselves. Hong Kong was the Mecca of retail therapy and we indulged in jewellery, clothes and rosewood furniture in particular. We had to do the jewellery bit twice because we suffered a burglary. The burglar entered the block of flats in the middle of the day and, strangely enough, there were no amahs about to raise the alarm!

The Naval Base at HMS TAMAR, apart from providing me with an office, also supplied the most wonderful food for parties. In one memorable period we were out nineteen evenings out of twenty-one. Impoverished naval officers had some difficulty in keeping up with their civilian counterparts but naval boats for beach picnics (banyans) were a very good way of returning hospitality *(Photo page 193)*.

One of our more indifferent moments concerned a certain Typhoon Rose. Over the eighteen months we had been in Hong Kong, we had experienced a number of typhoon warnings none of which had amounted to more than a big storm. We lived on what was known as the 'mid-levels' on the island overlooking the racecourse at Happy Valley. In fact we could see from our flat the racehorses being exercised on the Jockey Club roof; shortage of space in Hong Kong meant that every usable flat area had to be used! We had been invited to a party further along the mid-levels and, typhoon or no typhoon, we decided to go. We put up the typhoon shutters, left the amah in charge and drove off to the party. About midnight it became clear that this was no ordinary typhoon so we returned home, dodging the falling trees on the way. The amah had gone into a state of complete funk, as apparently the Chinese are wont to do during typhoons, but the children were fast asleep, so all was well.

Elsewhere in the harbour total turmoil prevailed. The winds had been up to 170 mph. Several American warships were high and dry on various islands, including an enormous troopship on its way to collect troops from Vietnam. The Royal Navy practice was to send all but the smallest ships to sea before the typhoon arrived. Our Commodore had advised the Americans accordingly but they chose to ignore his wise words. However, by far the greatest tragedy of Typhoon Rose was a mud-slide which brought down two very tall buildings at mid-levels causing over 200 fatalities.

Finding that running naval communications was not a very challenging occupation – with not very many ships – I took over the running of the Services sailing. On every visit since 1953, I had been given the standard Service's briefing on arrival in the Colony: "We are about to build a Services Water Sports Centre at Stanley on the south side of the Island." Twenty years or so later, nothing had happened. So, a Captain in the Irish Guards, Charles Aikenhead, who was a civil engineer by training, drew up the plans. I obtained the funds from my boss, Commodore Hong Kong. We summoned a Chinese building contractor and, six weeks later, it was finished. A beautifully printed invitation card was sent to the Commander British Forces inviting him to perform the Opening Ceremony complete with press, gin and tonic and tape for cutting. The invitation caused the General's staff to go into a complete panic because they had never heard of the project. However the Opening Ceremony was duly carried out with good grace: I had to ration my visits to the Headquarters for a few weeks.

The Stanley Services Boat Club needed an event to announce its arrival to the Services and sailing worlds. After the closure of the Naval Base at Singapore a large number of dinghies were sent up to Hong Kong, many of which were Bosuns, a boat carried by many an RN ship. So we decided to hold the World Bosun Dinghy Championships, with 54 boats competing. The RN Sailing Association championships in Portsmouth never had more than 20 boats. The Royal Yachting Association and the RNSA both agreed that the event could be held under their rules. Trying to get 54 boats measured was no small task. Three races were held in windy conditions and the first three places were taken by members of the Stanley Services Boat Club. I felt, as prime mover behind this initiative, that all our work had been justified. Incidentally we were sponsored by Johnny Walker whisky, I had personally probably consumed enough of the stuff to merit a bit of sponsorship.

Allens and Aikenheads teamed up once more to acquire a small, 24-foot junk for one hundred pounds. This vessel had gone to the bottom during Typhoon Rose. Basically 40 inches of rain was too much for it, so

Manager Major Jim Dunstone, Royal Artillery, receives the Bosun's Cup on behalf of the ANZUK team from Lt Col Tony Davis, Commanding Officer of 1st Battalion The Kings Regiment and Commodore of Stanley Services Boat Club

it settled down onto the mud of Aberdeen Harbour, the fishing port on the south side of the Island. The owner had arranged for it to be hoisted out, and we examined it there. It was fitted with a Petter diesel engine which turned over at the first try, in spite of having been underwater for six weeks. So we decided to buy it and arranged for it to be towed round to the other side of the Island to the Naval Base. We managed to organise for the cranes to be ready to lift the junk out on arrival, which was just as well as it was very near to making another expedition to the bottom of Hong Kong harbour.

Restoring the boat to working condition, fitting a junk style lugsail and providing basic amenities was accomplished for about £500. On completion, we motored and sailed round to the Stanley Services Boat Club where the Vice Commodore (me) had reserved a mooring. Even though it wasn't the speediest thing afloat, this junk provided great pleasure by way of beach parties, day and night bathing parties (some with skinny dipping, not a common practice in those days).

(See photographs on Pages 193-195).

Of course no stay in Hong Kong would be complete without a visit to the Portuguese colony of Macau, up the Canton River. The hydrofoils took you there in thirty minutes or so. Macau was a great attraction to the Chinese because of its casinos. The Chinese are inveterate gamblers. We went to look at the facades of the old Portuguese colonial houses, and for a change of scene from Hong Kong *(photo page 195).*

The Sultan of Brunei in North Borneo asked the Commodore, Hong Kong to carry out an inspection of his Navy. This consisted essentially of six Vosper-built fast patrol boats capable of 60 knots. I was part of the team which flew down for four days for this little adventure. Steaming around at night without lights at high speed, we succeeded in scaring ourselves silly, whereas the Brunei Navy were very much accustomed to such antics. Who did the Sultan of Brunei consider to be his enemies? The Malaysians, who had their eyes on his oil rigs.

Since this visit, Brunei has progressed from third world to first world status, thanks to the Sultan of Brunei's oil wealth and generosity towards his people *(photos page 196-197).*

One saddening event during our time in Hong Kong concerned the demise of the liner Queen Elizabeth I. The Chinese shipping magnate CY Tung purchased the ship at the end of its service in the UK and had it towed to Hong Kong. The idea was to turn it into a floating university. For some reason or other, it caught fire and the resultant pall of black smoke hung over the island for some time. Eventually the ship turned turtle and lay resting on the sea bottom. (*See Photograph on Page 197*).

On a return visit to Hong Kong in 2002, it was very difficult to find anything familiar, except the tram up the Peak. The naval base, HMS TAMAR, was occupied by the Chinese army.

Our stay in Hong Kong from 1971 to 1973 was one of the happiest periods for me and the family. It is worth pointing out that 36 years later many of those serving in the Navy in Hong Kong during our time still have the occasional reunion. It is not often that spontaneous and lasting friendships are achieved in this way.

Japanese Temples at Kyoto

Author at Kyoto Temple

Join the Navy, see the world?

In my Aide de Camp uniform outside the married quarters with Han Suyin house in background

Youngest son William with the car used to open the first road tunnel between Hong Kong Island and Kowloon, in front of Han Suyin house

Our junk (Platypus) at anchor off Stanley Beach

HK Harbour taken from The Peak, 1972

Open air market, Kowloon

Chinese fishing junk

Tai Pak floating restaurant

Postcard of Macau (tall building on right was our hotel)

The mosque, Brunei 2010

Postcard of Kampong Ayer, Brunei, 1978

View of the burnt out liner Queen Elizabeth I

"Meon Maid", the establishment yacht

HMS TIGER at Kielerwoche, 1976

Annual Anglo-German memorial service, 1975

BRITANNIA in the Kiel Canal

Join the Navy, see the world?

Chapter 20
HMS MERCURY
May 1973 to April 1974
Lieutenant-Commander

Responsibility for training communications and electronic warfare ratings at the Signal School, HMS MERCURY, was not perhaps a prime appointment but, after two years in Hong Kong, it provided an opportunity to settle back into life in England, and to live at home for once.

Apart from the work, I was also in charge of the Officers' shoot and the establishment yacht. The latter was a Northney 34, very similar to the better known Nicholson 34, but slightly heavier in build. More about these activities later.

The Electronic Warfare Branch had recently been created. The Navy was beginning to appreciate that the interception of enemy transmissions was a vital ingredient of fighting a ship in modern warfare and therefore needed to be integrated with the other functions of the Operations Room, e.g. anti-submarine, gunnery etc. So, shortly after I took up my job at MERCURY, the responsibility for training electronic warfare officers and ratings was transferred elsewhere so that a degree of integration with other warfare arms could be achieved.

However that left me responsible only for training communications ratings. As the Navy's communications gradually became semi-automated and with satellite communications more widely fitted, the place of the communications rating was becoming ever more irrelevant, both at sea and ashore. What was needed was a rating trained to both operate and maintain the radio equipment, but any proposals I made along these lines were firmly suppressed at the Signal School. I still had the job of keeping the young sailors being trained motivated, which I believe we did.

It is worth explaining at this stage how the Royal Navy was organised to fight a war at sea, very much as it had been in World War II. The Gunnery Department looked after guns and missiles, the Torpedo and Anti-Submarine Department looked after sonar and anti-submarine weapons and so forth. A ship needed to be able to react to multiple threats – missile, air or submarine – in a matter of seconds. This was not going to happen unless the officers and key ratings were trained accordingly.

In 1974 the Warfare Branch was formed, a move initiated by the First Sea Lord, a very able officer indeed. This eventually meant the end of the "tribal" organisation and the disappearance of the gunnery, torpedo and anti-submarine and communication branches. Needless to say this re-organisation of the method of fighting ships at sea was bitterly resented by several naval establishments. When promoting what have since proved very necessary changes, I too became pretty unpopular, particularly at the Signal School. I frequently ask why the Navy as a whole had taken so long to reach these conclusions. I wouldn't claim to be a visionary but I had realised that this needed doing many years earlier.

The Communications Branch had a very distinguished patron, Lord Louis Mountbatten. He usually attended the annual Signal Officer's Reunion at HMS MERCURY and did so in 1974. After supper I was summoned:

Lord Louis: "David, has he got it right?" – gesturing in the direction of the First Sea Lord.

Little pause for thought while I realised the import of the question.

Self: "I hope so, Lord Louis, otherwise we'll all be in trouble", which seemed to fit the bill. To be asked my opinion of the merit of the First Sea Lord's re-organisation of the Navy's fighting capability did not make me feel entirely comfortable. Afterwards I realised that I had been selected for this question because I had recently written a paper that more or less suggested that communications ratings should be found a more useful function on board ship.

The Ministry of Defence succeeded in selling the latest electronic warfare detection equipment to the Iranian and Argentinean navies, and we were thus responsible for teaching them how to use it. So will the Iranians be our next enemies at sea?

You will realise from the above that I was gradually working myself out of a job. So I had plenty of time to spend sailing the establishment yacht, complete with dedicated skipper *(photo page 198)*. The boat was kept at Whale Island, by the ferry terminal in Portsmouth. This was a chance to return hospitality by inviting friends to sail during Cowes Week. It blew storm force throughout the week, but while virtually all the newly designed lightweight boats in Class 4 were either de-masted or blown ashore or both, the Meon Maid, well reefed down, steamed on. Many of the guests were horribly sick but we actually won Class 4. My lesson from this week was that a good skipper is the answer to this yacht racing game, and maybe you have to pick your crew more carefully.

One afternoon at Cowes we finished very early so we went up to the teleprinter kiosk to see the results being printed off. From the rear: "Stand aside Class One here," Edward Heath in full voice. From the front: "Stand aside Class 4 here", yours truly. Prime Minister he may have been but such boorishness was inexcusable.

I organised a trip across the Channel to the Normandy coast in the Meon Maid with another family from Hong Kong days. On the way over we filled the stern sheets with mackerel which, on arrival at Honfleur, we exchanged with the local fishermen for a bag of mussels. It was extremely rough on the return trip which I fear put some people off sailing for life. It was the day when Edward Heath's Morning Cloud sank with the loss of several crew.

I mentioned the Signal Officer's shoot earlier. For my last few months at MERCURY, I ran this activity. This was a good excuse to escape from amending syllabi some of the time. We had a rewarding season with several record bags, which proved that our summer pheasant feeding programme had been well directed.

At the end of 1974 I learnt formally that I was not going to be promoted to Commander. It was a bit dispiriting for a few days but then I received some very good news.

Chapter 21
Kiel, Germany & Karup, Denmark
May 1974 to May 1977
Commander

Barely having failed to be promoted to Commander, I was offered a three year appointment to the NATO Headquarters at Kiel, West Germany as an Acting Commander. Great news, particularly from a financial point of view; not only was I assured of a Commander's pension, but I would also receive a large contribution towards school fees for three years. Furthermore, it was relatively easy to attend the two elder children's school events in the UK.

Let me start this episode in my naval career by explaining what NATO aimed to achieve in the mid 1970's. It was the height of the Cold War and the East German border was a mere 30 miles away from Kiel. A large number of Russian tanks with East German crews could be at our front door in a matter of hours. Only a nuclear device would stop them, or maybe the unwillingness of East Germans to fight their fellow countrymen? So NATO was designed to provide a barrier from Northern Norway as far south as Turkey. The task of the Commander Naval Baltic Approaches (COMNAVBALTAP – my friends thought I had joined a plumbing firm!) was to command the German and Danish navies on the outbreak of war - not very realistic. I could never see either the Germans or the Danes ceding control of their forces to such a multi-national and barely cohesive affair. The Commanding Admiral alternated between Denmark and Germany, and the rest of the Staff consisted of 5 Germans, 3 Danes, 1 US, 1 Canadian and 2 British officers, plus my Communications Centre staff of four ratings.

I was frequently being called upon to attend conferences and courses and visited Oberammergau, in southern Germany, Brussels and Norfolk, Virginia during the first two years, using up the NATO travel budget to good advantage. Lots of multi-national seminars were held within these conferences, giving an excellent opportunity to see how different nationalities viewed the world, the Soviet threat, and other military problems. Most occasions were dominated by the American doctrine, after all they really funded NATO and supplied a large part of the forces and equipment.

As Senior British Officer in Kiel, I was required to officiate at the annual NATO/German memorial service *(photo page 199)*. In the photo, the person on the right in a dark grey suit is Admiral Doenitz, Hitler's naval commander-in-chief, who, after serving his prison sentence, retired to live in Kiel.

NATO celebrated every national holiday, which meant that in effect one only worked about half the year. However, in between times, COMNAVBALTAP held a live exercise using Danish and German ships each year. Composite communications orders, so beloved of the Germans - General Montgomery said: "Rules are for fools and Germans" – had been written in the Headquarters. Any deviation from these orders was regarded by the Germans as a form of Anglo-Saxon treachery, so my plans to try something radically different came to nothing. I intended to run the exercise using no active radar or radio transmissions, knowing that the Russians were quite capable of intercepting everything and storing it away for jamming in the event of conflict. However my proposals were deemed too radical. I mention this because I have found that it is typical of the German mindset, in both commercial and military spheres. They will implement written instructions to the letter, regardless of whether it is sensible to do so or not. In fact, many Germans will not take any action until they receive written instructions.

The social and domestic life at Kiel was of a superior quality. We lived in a house that had been a German Admiral's residence during World War II, and had a putzfrau (cleaning lady) to go with it. We used British Army facilities, primary schools and the NAAFI shop. Fairly generous overseas allowances and duty-free booze made for a pleasant existence.

Rosemary & myself attending NATO Communications Ball, Bonn 1976

We made a number of skiing expeditions to St Anton in Austria where the family became reasonably competent skiers. I also had two trips to the Hartz Mountains for the same purpose under the title of "adventurous training" and therefore free of charge. We also had generous allowances of duty-free petrol to enable us to travel around Germany.

The sailing facilities at Kiel were really good. The British Kiel Yacht Club was only a mile away, so I imported an Achilles 24 yacht which slept 4 and was towable. We spent many pleasant days sailing round the western end of the Baltic. Three years prior to our arrival the Olympic sailing regatta had been held at Kiel Schilksee, five miles up the road. Each year Kielerwoche (Kiel Week), the German equivalent of Cowes Week, was held in the Kielerfjord *(photo page 198)*. Kielerwoche was an annual high point with yachts from many countries taking part. This particular year an American warship was berthed next to one from the Royal Navy. The Americans put a large sign next to their gangway with the ship's motto: "Second to none" clearly visible to all. Quick as a flash, an even larger sign appeared at the RN ship's gangway – "None". On another occasion much effort went into chartering suitable vessels upon which the visiting naval VIP's were to be lavishly entertained while watching the racing. Sadly there wasn't a breath of wind and not a single competitor ruffled the glassy sea all day. In 1976, the World Finn, Laser and OK dinghy championships were included in this regatta. Several of the world's top dinghy sailors camped out on us. Furthermore our eldest son, Tim, had acquired an OK dinghy and was able to take part in the OK world championship. He came eleventh at the age of 16!

One of our near neighbours at Kiel was Hans Hass, a retired German Naval U-boat commander who was credited with having sunk more Allied shipping than any other U-boat captain. He was a delightful man who was very attached to the British in spite of his wartime exploits. He very much enjoyed making fun of his own race and had a great fund of stories about German follies.

The Kiel Canal *(photo page 199)*, built in the 1930's to enable the biggest German warships, BISMARK and TIRPITZ, to get from Kiel to the North Sea without going round the top of Denmark, is one of the great waterways of the world. We had plans to sail through it but never managed to do so. By walking through the woods adjacent to the house we could watch the ships, or at least the top half of them, passing through the Canal.

The Germans had always wanted to move the COMNAVBALTAP Headquarters to Denmark so that they could claim overseas allowances. Unfortunately for us their wish came true so the last ten months of my job were spent on a Danish Air Force base at Karup in the middle of Jutland. For a sea command this was totally unsuitable, but we were stuck with it. I was responsible for moving the British element of the Headquarters. I was required to liaise with the senior British officer at Karup, a certain Group Captain in the Royal Air Force. For furnishing our hirings, we were each given an allowance. Rather than letting us do this in our own way, said Group Captain arranged with a local contractor to supply everything with no choice of furniture being left to us. He forgot to tell us that he was receiving a backhander from the Danish supplier! When I discovered this, I telephoned the Second Sea Lord who was due to visit us shortly and appraised him of the circumstances. He brought his visit forward. Within 24 hours the Group Captain was in an aeroplane on his way home to avoid embarrassing the British presence in NATO with a court martial.

We lived in a house overlooking a lake in a small town called Viborg, which was 20 miles from the air base. The whole of Jutland was covered in snow and ice for six months, so driving to and fro was hazardous. Watching the ice yachts on the lake from our drawing room window was good entertainment.

As it was mainly winter, we perhaps didn't get the best impression of living amongst the Danes. Very short days meant that most of the entertainment was indoors. One would have to say that excessive mindless drinking coupled with a degree of pornography seemed to be the norm. Unlike at Kiel, we never became properly integrated, really for the first time abroad, despite R giving English lessons to the ladies from the cathedral and plying them with traditional British, homebaked cakes. It was common knowledge that most Danish households had large white sheets ready to hang out in the event of a Soviet invasion – nothing new there then!

Reflecting on three years at a NATO Headquarters I would say that it was a very good thing that NATO was never really tested by the Soviets. The co-operation between the nations was minimal (cf Afghanistan more recently?). If the Soviets had decided to invade West Germany, the only way of stopping them would have been to press the nuclear button. I cannot see how approval would have been gained for that to happen.

Very early on after my arrival in COMNAVBALTAP, I ordered that only British personnel would be allowed to enter the Communication Centre. That included the boss, the Danish Admiral. One day I had overheard a German Navy Captain on our staff speaking on the telephone in our Headquarters to his family in East Germany. It was obvious to me that security in the Headquarters was tenuous to say the least, blood probably being thicker than the NATO alliance. Having said that, day-to-day life in the Headquarters was generally convivial, and usually consisted of planning the next excursion! (Not for nothing was it often called the 'North Atlantic Travel Organisation'!)

There is no doubt that common NATO procedures, based on American ones, did enable ships to operate together at sea. Certainly the US Navy and the Royal Navy have usually worked effectively together. A more or less common language helps a lot. However, all that is not much use unless you share the same objectives and have an agreed view of the enemy. NATO navies were never tested in Europe and probably won't be now. In 1975-77 the best way to describe the combined German and Danish navies would be largely ineffective. This was particularly so because the Danes and the Germans had little love for one another. Maybe, if threatened under wartime conditions, they might have co-operated.

The children obtained a lot of enjoyment from my three-year sojourn in NATO, with extended trips around Europe, sailing and skiing. But three years of a fairly mindless professional existence was enough for me.

Chapter 22
Admiralty Surface Weapons Establishment, Portsmouth
June 1977 to February 1978
Lieutenant-Commander

My last appointment in the Royal Navy was in Commander Naval Operational Command Systems (CNOCS). I can't really remember what this meant, but we were a small team of specialists deciding how new equipment being introduced at sea should be operated. My particular task concerned electronic warfare intercept equipment and jammers. We were based at the Above Surface Weapons Establishment on Portsdown Hill outside Portsmouth, about 20 minutes from home.

At that time we were busy commissioning new ships with intercept equipment that I had seen demonstrated twenty years previously, typical of the completely hopeless weapon system procurement process enjoyed by the Ministry of Defence. The procurement scientists altered the system specification so often that the manufacturers never got round to supplying the equipment to be fitted in ships.

I demonstrated my enthusiasm for this appointment by sending in a letter asking for voluntary retirement that was duly accepted. However I had to serve a further six months before I was allowed to depart finally. After three very enjoyable years as an Acting Commander it was very difficult to envisage what future appointments would be challenging enough to hold my interest. I will never forget how my father, a retired Army Lieutenant-Colonel, reacted when I told him I was going to leave the Navy:

Father: "What are you going to do?"

Self: "I'm going into the computer industry with a friend."
Father: "I can't understand why you would want to go into trade."
Self: "Three generations have been in the Services and, honestly, the cupboard is bare."

As you can imagine such an observation was not well received, but I think is typical of the experience of many families with a long tradition of being in the Services.

My boss at CNOCS was a charming guy who had been a midshipman with me in CEYLON. I persuaded him to send me on a series of courses designed to prepare me for my next career. First, a three-week computer course, then a three-week management course run by some management consultants in London, and a one-week course run by Olivetti demonstrated how ruthless commercial sales operations can be. All proved useful in the long run.

While serving out my time I did have an opportunity to go and see electronic warfare equipment that was being developed in other places. There was a truly memorable trip to Naples to see an incredible device that the American Navy was putting to sea. In this destroyer's operations room they had what looked like a television screen hooked up to a global chain of satellites. You paged through the associated computer system to find the part of the world that you wanted to look at. We chose the Black Sea where half the Soviet Navy was based. Zoom into Odessa. Zoom into the carrier MINSK. You could read the name MINSK on the cap tally of a Russian sailor walking on the flight deck of the carrier. Today, with Google, that doesn't surprise anyone but this was 1977. Equipment like this raises all sorts of interesting questions. Virtually any target anywhere in the world can be "illuminated", allied to a weapon, nothing is safe wherever it may be. We have seen how predator drones controlled from the USA can attack targets in Pakistan, presumably using the same sort of satellite technology. At present only the Americans are capable of deploying this type of system, but in due course others will be able to. Allied to a nuclear capability, the possible outcomes are too horrendous to contemplate.

How secure are the satellites used to control these systems? Perhaps that was the reason the Americans were so keen to develop their "star wars" technology, although, I rather suspect they already have addressed this. A few weeks before I left the Navy I thought I would write to the Admiral in charge of weapons procurement whom I knew quite well. The letter went along the following lines:

"Dear Admiral,
As I will be leaving the Royal Navy shortly I wanted to write to you personally to express my views regarding something I am very concerned about.
As you know the UAA1 (Electronic Warfare Intercept equipment) is widely fitted in frigate-size ships upwards. It is programmed ashore to intercept only Soviet emissions. With my newly acquired computer knowledge, I believe it would be possible to train the operators to re-programme this equipment to meet any new threat e.g. from the Iranians or Argentineans possibly.
I hope you will appreciate the extent to which the security of our ships could be improved by introducing this measure.
Yours sincerely."

Reply:
"Dear David,
Sorry to hear you are leaving the Navy. I am afraid we don't have the resources to implement your proposals at present but we will certainly give it consideration in future planning.
Yours sincerely."

Whether any of the seven ships sunk in the Falklands War by Argentine Exocet missiles five years later would have been saved we shall never know, but it seems reasonable to suppose that some might.
HMS MERCURY, the Signal School, very kindly dined me out before I collected my 'bowler hat' (naval expression). By this time I hardly knew any of the officers there. In my after dinner talk I tried to paint a picture of what it was like to join the Navy at the age of thirteen in 1949 in comparison with the Navy of today. I fear my talk, though lasting only a few minutes, fell on deaf ears. 'It don't blow like it used to blow' is often

not well received!

I managed to organise an almost seamless transition to civilian life by arranging that my computer systems house had a couple of small contracts for the Navy.

Chapter 23
Career Reflections

My career, from May 1949 until the end of 1977, saw the Royal Navy contract from the immediately post-war worldwide deployment – 6 fleets, 500 ships and half a million men – to one, essentially home-based fleet, with 50 ships and 90,000 men and women.

In 1949, the Royal Navy was second only to the Americans in size and was capable of supporting simultaneously United Nations and Empire requirements almost anywhere. After Korea (1953), the need to fight powerful conventional naval enemies seemed to have disappeared. As the Empire contracted, the Royal Navy had to do likewise, noting that many ships had been built for the Second World War and were less than ten years old. The majority of officers and men had trained for a full career and many found themselves 'surplus to requirement'. They were given gratuities to retire known as 'golden bowlers', but they were not really very generous. The disruption this caused at many levels was very evident.

By 1977, the Royal Navy was a smaller service than the one I joined in 1949, Officers commanded much more by dint of their intellectual ability than in previous times. The method of operating a ship in wartime conditions with multiple threats, principally missile, had changed so that all specialisations, gunnery, torpedo anti-submarine, electronic warfare and helicopters were learning to function in harmony. All this before women went to sea!

Upon reflection I realise what an enormous privilege it was to serve in the Royal Navy for 28 years. When, as a small boy, I elected to try and become a Naval Officer, I informed the assembled Board of Admirals that I was attracted to life in the Royal Navy and that I wanted to travel. Well, I had a very happy life for most of my naval career and I certainly travelled, spending over 11 years East of Suez.

I suppose some would consider my time in the Navy as somewhat hedonistic and selfish. I missed large parts of family life, the birth of my children and seeing them grow up. On the other hand, we were able to enjoy many exotic places as a family. I have deliberately not made a lot of mention of the family in this essentially naval story, but without them much would not have been possible, or as enjoyable.

Even though I never achieved senior rank, I had a thoroughly enjoyable career as a Naval Officer, and you can't say fairer than that.